CW01637588

ALL ABOUT Opaline and Opaline Cinnamon Budgerigars

by

Roy Stringer
and
Fred Wright

First Published 1994

ISBN 0 9518145 6 7

Typeset in New Century Schoolbook and Printed in Britain by Spottiswoode Ballantyne, Colchester, Essex, England. Published by Roy Stringer Publications, Somerdale Cottage, Station Road, Westbury, Shropshire.

CONTENTS

Acknowledgements

Roy Stringer and Fred Wright gratefully acknowledge the kindness of Eric Peake in offering us the idea for this series of books and for painting the lovely Opaline Cinnamon Budgerigar on the cover, the great effort put in by Les Lockey, himself a very successful champion breeder, exhibitor and judge of Budgerigars, in travelling around Britain to take photographs of the experts, their birdrooms and – most importantly – their superb Opaline and Opaline Cinnamon Budgerigars specifically for this book, Harry Bryan, for delving into his wonderful memory to recall some outstanding Budgerigar of these varieties from the past, Steve Amos for using his special knowledge to supply a chapter on the special characteristics of the Opaline mutation, Brian Byles, Editor of *Cage & Aviary Birds* and Peter Moss, Editor of *Bird keeper* for their support and advice during the book's preparation and Bruce Cole, in South Africa, for his help in obtaining Dr Robertson's contribution. Then, of course, there are the experts who have answered dozens of questions in our quest to discover what it is that has brought them success at the highest levels with Opaline and Opaline Cinnamon Budgerigars; Eric and Michael Lane, Jim Hutton, Roy Aplin and Dr Alf Robertson. We thank them all.

The intention of the authors* of this book is to address the decline in quality and numbers of exhibition Opaline and Opaline Cinnamon Budgerigars by offering a platform for some of the world's most successful breeders of these varieties so that they can reveal their techniques, methods, likes, dislikes and hopes for the future. We sincerely hope we will succeed. The experts have not been "led" when answering the comprehensive range of questions put to them and editing has been kept to the minimum required. After studying their answers, readers might like to look for the reasons behind each expert's success and try to do their own part in bringing Opalines and Opaline Cinnamons back to their former glory.

You will not find the colour standards or scale of points of any organisation – for more than one reason. Different countries have different standards. There is a distinct possibility that an international standard could be agreed before the end of the century. If you want to read a particular club's standards you can join the club – the space in this book is better devoted to the opinions of the breeders who have proved their ability by winning at the very highest levels. Colour standards and points allocations vary from country to country, but an outstanding Budgerigar is recognised the world over.

**(Roy Stringer, formerly a design engineer in the motor industry, is Features Editor of CAGE & AVIARY BIRDS. Fred Wright, once a teacher, is now a freelance avicultural consultant to several companies and a regular contributor of articles to CAGE & AVIARY BIRDS and other avicultural magazines. Both are successful champion breeders and exhibitors of Budgerigars and international judges.)*

FOREWORD

by Eric Peake

Opalines first appeared in the exhibition Budgerigar Fancy in the early 1930s. They were a wonderful addition to the fairly limited range of varieties of the time. The Cinnamon mutation had appeared just before and it must have been a very excited breeder who first saw the result of combining the two varieties to create the Opaline Cinnamon.

Over the years, Opalines have been used to improve other varieties and this has caused marking faults to appear on the Opalines produced in the process. These same marking faults have been transferred to Opaline Cinnamons and that is why both Opalines and Opaline Cinnamons are included in the same book.

Opalines

A true Opaline Budgerigar is a beautiful bird, but they are few and far between, these days. The clarity of the head and saddle (between the wing butts) combined with the brilliant opalescent body colour, which was also repeated as a background colour on the wings, made it distinctly different from the Normal Budgerigar. Today, there are Opalines that are virtually indistinguishable from Normals.

The most common marking faults to be seen on even the best Opalines today, are the result of intensifying the same black markings that made Opalines such attractive mates for increasing the mask spot size on Normals. It is very rare indeed to see an exhibition Opaline that does not have the fault of a "dirty back" (the presence of black markings on what should be a clear "V" between the wing butts). Head flecking (black marks on what should be a clear white or yellow head) spoils many Opalines that are otherwise good exhibition specimens. Multi-spotted Opalines can require so much mask trimming that the result is a moth-eaten appearance.

When the amount of black marking is reduced, the result can be the serious fault known in the old days as "thumb prints" - wings that are too lightly marked. Patchy body colour, on chest, rump and vent areas, is another fault to be avoided. During the early and mid-1970s I had a successful stud of Opaline Grey Greens and I found that the best results were achieved from Opaline to Opaline pairings.

Good examples of Opalines have been absent from the show bench for many years. Those who can recall the magnificent Opaline Violets exhibited by Bill Watmough and the outstanding Opaline Greys of Tommy Rothery know what wonderful Budgerigars Opalines can be.

Opaline Cinnamons

Due to their Cinnamon content, Opaline Cinnamons are often used by breeders to produce softer, finer feathering. Being sex-linked in their mode of inheritance, both Opaline and Cinnamon can be carried hidden by cocks and so newcomers to the hobby are often warned to be careful in their use, as their numbers can increase more quickly than intended.

All Budgerigar colours appear in three different shades; light, medium and dark. In Greens they appear as Light Green, Dark Green and Olive. However, when the Grey factor is involved (in Greys and Grey Greens) it is not always obvious which category of shade a particular birds falls into by studying its body colour alone. However, the cheek patch always gives an indication. On Opaline Cinnamon Greys and Opaline Cinnamon Grey Greens the differences are more marked. For example, an Opaline Cinnamon Grey Green of light shade has a silvery cheek patch. Its medium counterpart has a cheek patch which is blue/grey and an Opaline Cinnamon Grey Green of dark shade has a dark grey cheek patch.

One interesting feature of Opaline Cinnamons is that pairing light factor birds together (Light Green x Light Green, Light Green x Skyblue or Skyblue x Skyblue) can result in weak-coloured progeny, with respect to both body and wings. This makes Dark-factor Budgerigars (particularly Dark Greens and Cobalts) valuable when breeding Opaline Cinnamons. The use of Opaline Cinnamon Grey Greens and Opaline Cinnamon Greys also overcomes this tendency to lose depth of colour.

In the 1980s, I particularly admired the Opaline Cinnamons of the Green series bred by Roy Aplin and those of the Blue series bred by Eric and Michael Lane. These breeders are among the experts who put forward their views in this book.

INTRODUCING THE OPALINE MUTATION

by Steve Amos

History has it that the first Opaline mutation appeared in 1934, in the form of one unusually-marked chick in a nest of Normal Cobalts. The parents were a Normal Skyblue and a Normal Mauve.

These Cobalts were bred by a Mr A. Brown, of Kilmarnock in Scotland, who described the unusual youngster as being almost devoid of black barring (now called undulations) on the head, neck and back. The frontal and crown of the head were pure, unmarked white. The body colour was an intense, bright Cobalt throughout, as were the back of the neck and the area between the wing butts. The markings on the wings were black (like its Normal nest mates) but what had been the white areas had changed to an iridescent suffusion of bright, intense cobalt; the same colour as the body. This stranger-in-the-nest was a hen and at first was called a "Pied".

By its first breeding season it was in the possession of Mrs Ashby, of Ayr (also in Scotland), - and produced only Normal chicks; cocks and hens. The following year, the original "Pied" hen was paired with its own sons and produced "Pieds"; both cocks and hens. What we now know as the Opaline mutation had been established - though it would seem that its name was changed again; to "Marbled".

In 1936, the strain of "Marbleds" was acquired by Mr W.E. Higham (the president of the Budgerigar Society (BS), that year) whose aviary manager was Len Hillas (who was awarded the BS Silver Bird, in recognition of his service to the Fancy, in 1949). It was, in fact, from the writings of Mr Hillas that much of this historical information has been gleaned. In the Higham aviaries, the new mutation's characteristics were combined with all of the existing black-eyed varieties and also with the Cinnamon mutation, to create Opaline Cinnamons.

Two other mutations - either the same or similar - appeared around the same time; in Australia and Belgium. The Australian form was found in a consignment of trapped, wild Budgerigars and established by Mr S.E. Terrill of Adelaide, South Australia. The Belgian expression of the mutation appeared in the aviaries of Mr L. Raymaekers, of Brussels. The genetic inheritance of all three strains seemed to operate in the same (sex-linked) way. Eventually, the name "Opaline" was coined in Australia and was recognised and accepted by the Budgerigar Society.

Although the three mutations of Opaline - the Scottish, Australian and Belgian - bred in the same way, it was noticeable that the Belgian form had much reduced wing markings and smaller mask spots. This could have been caused by being combined with Dilutes and Clearwings to produce an almost Self-coloured Budgerigar.

In the fourth edition of *Budgerigar Matings and Colour Expectations*, published by the BS in 1938, Cyril H. Rogers FZS, revealed that no standard of perfection for Opalines had yet been fixed. I believe a standard WAS written around 1939, and the fifth edition of the same book contains standards for Opaline Light Green, Dark Green, Olive, Skyblue, Cobalt, Mauve, Violet, Grey and Grey Green. Since then, there has been a series of Opaline standards published with changes, particularly to wing markings.

Wing Markings

Although it has always been stated that wing markings should be black on a body-colour background, examination of the Budgerigar Society's colour standard for Opalines, through the years, reveals that there have been slight changes to the requirements. The following table illustrates the point:

Year	ground colour	markings
1939	iridescent	normal and symmetrical
1952	iridescent	normal and symmetrical
1970	suffused iridescent	normal
1978/9	suffused opalescent	normal
1984	suffused opalescent	normal and symmetrical
1989	suffused opalescent	normal and symmetrical
1994	opalescent	symmetrically shaped

In the 1970s there was a long debate in the BS Council regarding the two words "opalescent" and "iridescent". As I recall, it took the best part of an afternoon, with opinion seeming to be equally divided. Some weight was given to the description of the first mutation, written in 1934, which asserted that "iridescent" was the correct description. The focus of debate turned to dictionary definitions and "opalescent" ("showing changing colours") won the day.

As can be seen from the table, the word "normal" has been in the Opaline wing standard from 1939 right up until it was dropped in 1994 – and it is a word that has caused problems. Some sections of the Fancy have blamed it for causing a drastic decline in the typical "Opaline" characteristics. It is said to be responsible for dark markings on the back of the neck and head (where it should be clear), for a reduction in the amount of body colour on wings and for losing the beautiful and distinctive clear "V" on the back, between the wing butts.

It is possible that the word "normal" has not been interpreted correctly. The intention, I am sure, was to describe the wing markings as being exactly the same in number and distribution as on the Normal variety.

"Thumb marks" or "smudging" (descriptive of patches of body colour being apparent on the wings) have caused controversy for many years – and will possibly do so for many years to come. It is a fact that it is easier to breed Opalines with clean backs if their wings are "thumb-marked" rather than displaying "normal" markings. I believe that the correct approach is not to take the easy route, but to persevere in trying to produce Opalines with clean backs and which comply with the written and pictorial standards, combined with the Scale of Points for the variety.

Tails

When "thumb-marks" were very prevalent, in the 1970s, there were lots of Opalines to be seen with "foul tails"; tails that were nearly all yellow or white. Up until then, the colour requirement on tail feathers was that they should not be lighter than the equivalent mantle colour. As a corrective, in 1984, the colour of Opalines' tail feathers were required to be the same as their Normal equivalents: eg. dark blue for Light Greens and black for Grey Greens.

Flecking

One of the biggest controversies in the Budgerigar Fancy, in the 1980s, involved head flecking and much of the controversy was caused by differences in interpretation or understanding of what constitutes flecking. So let me start be defining it. Flecking, constitutes any markings of any other colour, anywhere on a Budgerigar's yellow or white frontal or crown, that can be seen by the naked eye. And that applies to EVERY variety of Budgerigar.

It is inevitable that a book on Opaline Budgerigars should have a section on flecking, because the Opaline has been blamed for introducing this serious fault and spreading it to other varieties. I have to say that I have difficulty in accepting that point of view, wholeheartedly.

Another problem, when defining flecking, is that it varies in degree through all of the stages between being so dense that the whole frontal and crown appear to be black to fine marks (sometimes called "dust marks") that are almost invisible. But any degree of flecking can be defined as "small spots or tick marks which travel from FRONT TO BACK, in a direction from the cere to the back of the head. This is quite different from the natural head striations (narrow, striped markings) which travel SIDE TO SIDE, across the frontal. These do not constitute flecking. The short striations which appear above and forward of the centre of the eye should not be confused with flecking, although they ARE undesirable. Ideally, there should be no markings on the frontal or crown and the head striations should not begin forward of the eye. Some Budgerigars have the fault of a short cap, where the striations start forward of the eye. I do not believe that flecking is responsible for this fault.

At its height, the flecking controversy reached a stage where, at one show, a judge was seen lifting a Budgerigar's head feathers with a second judging stick, to see if he could find flecking. In my opinion, one stick is enough for any judge; a second should be banned.

As the flecking situation worsened, the Budgerigar Society decided that no flecked bird should be considered for a special award, but this did not solve the problem entirely. There were those on the General Council who felt that some judges could not, or would not, interpret or operate the show standards and directives correctly.

From the start of the 1986 show season, the BS decreed that no flecked bird could win a class. If there was only one bird in a class – and it was flecked – it must be placed second. This resulted in a situation, at some shows, where far less first prize winners than usual were brought forward to compete for the major awards. Throughout the controversy, I maintained the position that if judges are appointed they must be permitted to make decisions. Flecking is a fault and judges should take it into account and penalise it, in accordance with the severity of the flecking – just as they do with the many other faults displayed by exhibition Budgerigars. I am pleased to say that this approach was adopted and, in spite of an attempt to reintroduce the "no first prize" rule in 1991, remains the situation in 1994. Under these circumstances, I believe the number of flecked exhibits on the show bench is diminishing.

In 1987/8, on behalf of the BS Colour Standards committee, I was pleased to collaborate with artist Eric Peake in the production of a set of paintings depicting the correct colour and markings of 27 different varieties described in the Colour Standards. These paintings were approved by the committee late in 1988 and by the full General Council in May 1989. They were published in the 1989 BS Handbook as an aid to the better understanding of what is required of a perfect example of each variety.

In 1992, BS members were invited to submit ideas for alterations or extensions to the written colour standards and scale of points. Many responded with useful contributions and I was asked to prepare drafts for revised standards. Discussion of these went on throughout 1992 and 1993 and I was pleased to be associated with the production of the new colour standards, which were published in book form in May 1994 – and were very well received. The new colour standards state that "the frontal and crown should be clear and free from all markings".

It remains to be seen what effect the new standards will have on the quality of future exhibits, or the way they will be judged, but if the end product is more Budgerigars being bred and exhibited that display 100 per cent Budgerigar quality plus 100 per cent variety content, the hard work and cost will all have been worthwhile. As far as Opalines are concerned, standards have been fixed for all nine basic colours in all established varieties, including Clearbodies.

Harry Bryan looks back

■ *Harry Bryan is the most successful Budgerigar fancier the world has ever known. He began keeping Budgerigars in 1916 and is still enjoying success on the show bench. In the intervening years he saw all of the top Budgerigars in the UK which until recently, in Budgerigar terms, meant the world. His memory is as keen as ever and here he recounts his memories of Opalines and Opaline Cinnamons.*

In September 1931, I was on honeymoon in Boscombe – not too far from where I now live. I went into a pet shop and spotted a small cage containing three hens. At first glance they might have been mistaken for Greywings, which had been around for just over 10 years at the time, but their markings were brown rather than grey. These were the first Cinnamon Budgerigars I ever saw. I bought all three for less than 50p and put them on the train to my hometown of Leamington, where my brother collected them from the station.

A couple of years later, the first-ever Opaline, an Opaline Cobalt, appeared in a nest in Scotland. It was bought by Sid Golland, a Southport scrap-dealer for £100 – at a time when £5 a week was a good wage. Sid exhibited the Opaline Cobalt at Sheffield show and took best in show. It was W.K.(Bill) Cox, one-time chairman and president of the Budgerigar Society, who took me to see my first Opaline; at the aviaries of a Mr Merritt in Smethwick. I was very friendly with a chemist who lived in Wem, Shropshire and he let me have two young Opaline Skyblue cocks, so it was not long before I was breeding Opalines. Soon after, I crossed them with my Cinnamons and was doing well with Opaline Cinnamons. Once they were established, Opalines were not specially expensive. I remember buying an Opaline Blue hen from the sales class at a show for £4 and breeding nine winners from her. One of them took the best-in-show award at the Budgerigar Society Club Show! One of my greatest achievements, with Opalines, came in 1956 when my Opaline Dark Green cock beat every other type of bird at the National Exhibition to win me the Supreme Trophy for the first time. I repeated the performance 20 years later with a Normal Grey. At one time I had 16 Opaline Grey Green cocks that were all capable of winning at championship shows – though the competition was not as fierce as it is today.

The first Opalines had wonderful markings and opalescent coloration and like every other Budgerigar variety that depends upon its markings for its unique beauty, it has suffered from being crossed indiscriminately with other varieties. I remember judging in Coventry with my friend and top Budgerigar breeder P.S.W.(Percy) Smith. Percy insisted that Opalines should have clean backs and any Opaline exhibit that had the slightest of markings between its wing butts was thrown out for "not being an Opaline". In one class he started with 14 exhibits and finished up with five! Eventually, he was forced to soften his attitude or there would have been no contenders for the best Opaline award. I recall having an argument, at a Budgerigar Society General Council meeting, with Ralph Frayne. Dirty backs were becoming evident and Ralph wanted the standard to call for Opalines with marble-like wings. He won the day but it did not cure the problem and the overall quality of Opalines suffered.

Later, the standard was changed to call for "Normal" wing markings and there are those who blame this for the problem of head flecking. I do not accept this, though the word "Normal" has now been removed from the standard. Today, the situation is far worse. There are Opalines with wings and backs that are indistinguishable from Normal's and Normals that carry so much body colour on their backs and wings that you have a job telling which is which. There is a positive aspect to all this. Because Opalines tend to have marking faults you can buy an Opaline of a given quality far more cheaply than a Normal of the same quality – and Opaline hens are the backbone of many a good stud.

I cannot recall anyone who stayed at the top with Opalines for long, but there are several that kept super Opaline Cinnamons for long periods of time. Smith & Wainwright, Mrs Angela Moss, Attwood & Hellier, Lane & Son and Jim Hutton (*the last two are featured in this book*) all fit into this category. Roy Aplin (*also featured in this book*) has some good ones and he always puts them onto the show bench in the absolute peak of condition. Perhaps the best of all were Smith & Wainwright's, but it was on their outstanding Opaline Cinnamons (mainly Light Greens with a little extra feather) that I first saw head flecking; albeit very slight. Although Opalines get the blame for introducing flecking to virtually every other variety, I blame Opaline Cinnamons. Because top breeders used outstanding, flecked Budgerigars in their breeding programmes the word soon spread that ALL flecked Budgerigars were useful in the breeding cage. This misconception caused much damage.

In my opinion, Opaline Cinnamons are very good starter birds for beginners. However, some writers have frightened them off by suggesting that they will get out of hand and over-run the other varieties in their studs. They need have no such fears. All that is needed is an understanding of the way that the Opaline and Cinnamon factors are inherited and this is explained simply in Chapter 7 of this book.

(*"The Budgerigar Man", the Harry Bryan story and way of breeding exhibition Budgerigars is available from the publishers of this book*)

MEET THE EXPERTS

ERIC AND MICHAEL LANE live in Royal Leamington Spa, England. Eric's father, Fred, joined the Budgerigar Society in 1935. The Lanes lived close to the great Harry Bryan and, during the Second World War, Fred went into partnership with Harry – breeding Dutch rabbits! When Fred rejoined the BS in 1949, Eric also caught the bug. Father kept Normals but the son fell in love with Opalines. From Harry Bryan he bought a pair of Opaline Blues, an Opaline Dark Green cock with an undershot beak and an Opaline Yellowface Grey hen with one good leg. They all bred! The partnership of F.N. Lane & Son was formed. In 1972, Fred Lane died and, at his wish, grandson Michael joined Eric to keep the Lane & Son partnership going – though being allergic to feather dust limits Michael's involvement. The following are just a few examples of the Lane's wins. Budgerigar Society Club Show: 1974; best breeder in show with an Opaline Grey cock: best Opaline for three consecutive years: 1978; best in show, best opposite sex and second best any age: 1979; second best breeder: 1983; best any age and best opposite sex: seven times best Opaline in show. National Exhibition since 1980: best in show seven times (three years running with the same Opaline Cinnamon Light Green cock, three times with Opaline cocks). Budgerigar World show: best in show twice with Opaline Grey Green cocks. At Area Championships, two wins stand out from many: best in show at both Lancashire, Cheshire & North Wales AND at Lincs & East Anglia with Opaline Cinnamon cocks – on the same week-end! "Lane" Budgerigars are known for being real show birds; excelling in feather quality and deportment. The answers that follow were compiled by Eric.

JIM HUTTON lives in Poole, a pleasant seaside town in the south-west of England. He is known for keeping a small select stud. Jim is a Scot and was living in Scotland when he first kept Budgerigars in partnership with his father – and when he started again in 1950. His first major win – best breeder in show – came in 1956 at East of Scotland show followed by best in show at Glasgow; both with Opaline Cinnamon cocks. His many Scottish wins included best in show at the Scottish National. Then, in 1960, he took a new job in Bristol. He soon realised that, his previous wins notwithstanding, if he wanted to compete with the excellent Budgerigars in the south he needed to rebuild his stud. Jim did not exhibit for three years, but when he returned he was soon on a winning streak. A series of local wins was followed by second best in show and best opposite sex at South Wales & Mons. area championship, then best opposite sex at the Budgerigar Society Club Show; both with Opaline Cinnamon Grey Green hens. Jim Hutton has also taken the BS Club Show trophies for second-best adult and second-best breeder. Other Hutton Opaline Cinnamon Grey Green hens took best in show awards at Bristol, Exeter and the Western Counties area championship. Another notable result, at the 1972 BS Club Show, was to take first and second place in all four champion Opaline Cinnamon classes. At Walsall BS championship show, he entered two young Opaline Cinnamon cocks, one in the any age class and the other in the breeder's. One took best breeder and the other best any age and best in show!

ROY APLIN lives in Wareham, Dorset, in the south of England. He started keeping Budgerigars when he was only 8 years old, but moved on to Canaries and British Birds before returning to his first love in 1969. Opalines were dominating the show scene at the time so it is not surprising that the Opaline mutation has always figured strongly in his stud. His first big win came when he was a beginner. Two of his Opaline Skyblue cocks took the best breeder and best in show awards in Bournemouth. As an intermediate, he bred an Opaline Cinnamon Grey Green which took best-in-show awards at four championship events before going to the Budgerigar Society Club Show and taking the trophies for best Opaline Cinnamon and best intermediate any age. At the first Budgerigar World show, in 1983, Roy's Opaline Cinnamon Grey Green cock took the best opposite sex in show award. The same cock was best in show, two years running at London & Southern Counties area championships. Two other outstanding Aplin Budgerigars, a Grey cock and a Skyblue cock, extended the run to unique proportions. Roy Aplin will always be remembered for taking the supreme award at London & Southern Counties for four consecutive years. He has registered several champion Budgerigars; four of them Opaline Cinnamons. Although trained as a carpenter/joiner, Roy Aplin has blossomed as a wildlife artist. He has been commissioned to paint pictures of Budgerigars by fanciers the world over. Because of his artistic approach, he looks at Budgerigars in a different way to most Budgerigar breeders; particularly with regard to feather structure.

Dr ALF ROBERTSON was the first South African Budgerigar fancier to gain world-wide recognition as a breeder. Over 70 years of age and still a practising doctor, he lives in Durban. "Doc" Robertson took up Budgerigars in the early 1950s and in 1955 bought a split Opaline cock from Ken Farmer of Luton, England; one of the few fanciers who can take credit for the quality of today's exhibition Budgerigars. The cock produced several good Opalines and Dr Robertson took up the challenge to improve them. His first South African championship win was with an Opaline Grey Yellow hen. Since then he has taken many top prizes, including best Budgerigar, best adult, best breeder and best opposite sex at the South African National Show. During his visits to South Africa, Brian Byles, Editor of *CAGE & AVIARY BIRDS*, became a firm friend of Dr Robertson and was amazed at the way that he could pair two "bucket-headed", heavily-flecked Opalines together to produce clean-headed winners. In spite of not having access to outcrosses from other countries for many years, (there was an import ban) Dr Robertson built up a stud that could hold its own with any other in the world. In the 1980s, Brian Byles admired a Robertson Grey Green cock that was best breeder and best in show at the South African National, so the "Doc" gave it to him. If evidence of the quality of the bird was needed, it could be found in the fact that it went on to take the best in show award, for Brian, at London & Southern Counties BS Area Championship show.

CHAPTER 1

THEIR BIRDROOMS

Describe your birdroom.

Eric and Michael Lane:

Michael is allergic to Budgerigar feather dust and has only a small birdroom at his home, where he is helped by his son, Ben. The main establishment is in my garden and consists of a main room (18ft x 12ft (5.5m x 3.6m)) with an extension (9ft x 12ft (2.7m x 3.6m)) and a separate small room which measures 8ft x 7ft (2.4m x 2.1m). The main room was built in the 1930s and consists of timber framing clad with asbestos. The floors are solid and covered with ceramic tiles. There are lots of windows which means that the temperature builds up at the height of summer. However, plenty of ventilation is provided by ventilators in the apex of the roof and having doors and windows open. The main room contains two 8ft x 4ft (2.4m x 1.2m) inside flights, side by side with the centre wall double-wired to avoid feet being pecked. Two 12ft x 4ft (3.6m x 1.2m) outside flights connect with the inside flights. The small room also has two inside and two outside flights. We sometimes use these for breeding pairs and they have produced some excellent Budgerigars. We have two sizes of breeding cage; 3ft (91cm)long and 2ft-6in (76cm) long. They are all located in the main room and its extension. There are 33 of the larger size and 15 of the smaller. We use external nest-boxes, 9in x 5in (23cm x 13cm), made from thick, resin-bonded plywood. Some have doors on their ends and others have doors on their sides. A 2in (5cm) thick concave is used to keep in the heat and a piece of plywood, tacked onto the end of the concave, stops chicks from falling out of the box. The most sophisticated piece of equipment is the automatic watering system; money well spent – though such systems need to be fitted properly. Having tried humidifiers and ionisers we no longer use them. The main, fluorescent lights are controlled by a time switch though the nightlights are switched manually from the house. Thermostatically-controlled electric heaters are used when the weather is very cold.

Jim Hutton:

Following recent alterations, my birdroom is now "L-shaped" with the main breeding cages facing south – which I feel is important if best results are to be achieved. The inside flight is also "L-shaped"; the long leg

Eric Lane just stands and looks, but inside his birdroom (below) his Budgerigars are breeding. The automatic watering system connected to each cage saves valuable time.

being 13ft long x 3ft-3in wide (4m x 1m) and the short leg 8ft-2in x 2ft (2.5m x 0.75m). The height is approximately 5ft (1.5m). The insertion of a slide, where the two legs meet, creates two useful flights. The smaller one is ideal for youngsters for the period between leaving their parents and being released into the outside flight. The inside flight is raised from the floor to provide storage space beneath. This is a great help in keeping the birdroom tidy. My breeding cages are large, by conventional standards, because I believe that the birds must have plenty of room to spread their wings if they are going to be breeding for five months of the year. The cages are built into the room's wall. Each cage measures 51in long x 18in high x 18in deep (1.3m x 0.5m x 0.5m). When slides are removed, three 20ft (6m) long flight cages are created. Opposite the short leg of the inside flight is a small, two-tier bank of cages; 8ft-2in (2.5m) long. They can be divided to form four smaller cages. These are used mainly for show preparation, young stock or even hospitalisation. In the southern-facing wall is a louvre window. Since the prevailing wind comes from that direction it is relatively simple to control the air intake, thus making sure that there is adequate ventilation. I believe this to be very important, particularly during the breeding season or spells of hot weather. I also have a very effective fan, which keeps the atmosphere in the birdroom bearable, even in the hottest weather. I used to consider large, outside flights to be important - but now I have changed my thinking. Modern Budgerigars, with their larger feathers, do not utilise flights as their finer-feathered ancestors did. So I recently incorporated a large proportion of the outside flight into the room itself. Extending the room in this way is one of the best decisions I have ever made. The outside flight that remains consists of three adjoining sections, forming a "Z" shape. The birds have a flying length of 28ft (8.5m), but not in a straight line. Flying around corners helps to develop their shoulder muscles, rather than their necks. Inside the room, everything is aimed at easy maintenance; glazed tiled walls, vynil tiled floor and the framing of the cages and flights in polished hardwood. I now intend to replace the punch-bar cage fronts with new, all-plastic versions. My external nest-box design is not at all conventional. It consists of a rectangular box (10in long x 8in deep x 5in wide (25cm x 20cm x12cm)) made from exterior plywood - 6mm for the sides and top, 12mm for the bottom. The entrance hole is 2in (50mm) in diameter and located near the top of the side which comes against the cage front. The top consists of a sliding panel, through which inspections are made. No concave is employed, but a 50mm layer of coarse sawdust is placed in the bottom - to be replaced if the hen throws it out. Each year the boxes are cleaned thoroughly and varnished inside and out. The varnish fills all cracks and crevices and so there are no mite in my nest-boxes. The level of equipment in the room is fairly basic. Two fluorescent tubes are controlled by a 24 hour timeswitch; set to give 1½ hours artificial light early morning, then to come on again ½ an hour before dusk and finally switching off at 10pm. An oil-filled electric radiator is controlled by a thermostat to come on if the room temperature drops below 36deg F (2deg C). An ioniser is used in the non-breeding season. When used in the breeding season it caused dust to collect on the nest-boxes closest to

Outside view of Jim Hutton's birdroom.

Inside Jim Hutton's birdroom showing the flight on one side, stock cages on the other, with good ventilation at the end.

it. All other functions are carried out manually. There is no running water or automatic watering system. The nightlight (a 6 watt fluorescent tube) is switched on manually. The advantage of this is it gives the opportunity for a final inspection before the main lights go out for the night.

Roy Aplin:

My birdroom is timber-framed with the walls clad with tongue-and-groove boarding and the roof and floor with plywood. It measures 22ft long x 8ft wide x 7ft high at the front (6.7m x 2.4m x 2.1m). The walls are lined with pre-painted hardboard, screwed into position with beading covering the joints. The space between the inner and outer walls is filled with fibre-glass insulation. The floor is tiled to facilitate cleaning. The metal-framed windows are fitted with frosted, Georgian, wired glass. Vents built into the walls provide ventilation. There are two inside flights - 9ft x 3ft (2.7m x 0.9m) and 6ft x 3ft (1.8m x 0.9m) - which extend from floor to ceiling. The smaller one connects to an outside flight which measures 12ft long x 6ft wide x 7ft high (3.6m x 1.8m x 2.1m). The perches are limited to one end of the outside flight and a felted roof keeps the sunshine off the birds when they are perching outside. There is a rotating perch at the other end. The floor is covered with pea gravel. The whole structure (birdroom and flights) is bolted together, rather then nailed or screwed because I believe that neither of those methods of fixing is strong enough. Back inside the room again, on the wall opposite the flights is a bank of 32 breeding cages, with storage cupboards beneath. The entrance door is in the middle of one end wall with the seed bin beside it. At the other end of the room is a tier of four cages, set at an angle so as not to restrict light from the main bank of cages. The main cages are set in four tiers, eight wide - built in three blocks so that they can be removed from the room. Each cage unit measures 30in long x 16in deep x 16in high (76cm x 41cm x 41cm). Each is equipped with one round and one square perch and a 3in (7.6cm) high front rail prevents seed husks from spilling onto the room's floor. The cage fronts are made from punch bar and chromium plated. There is a 6in x 6in (15cm x 15cm) removable door at the top corner which is removed when nest-boxes are fitted. Aluminium strips protect all corners. The cages are painted white. My nest-boxes are made from birch ply and are fixed to the outside of the cages by mirror brackets. The design incorporates a half-door for inspections, a 2in diameter (50mm) entrance hole with a perch beneath, an internal landing block and a concave. I have tried many types of nest-box and find this to be a practical design, though I am still thinking of changing to the box-within-a-box type. Taking into account the wide range of nest-box types used throughout the Fancy, it is apparent that Budgerigars in breeding condition will go to nest in almost any configuration. Main lighting is provided by three 5ft (1.5m) fluorescent tubes. Three low-wattage bulbs serve as nightlights. A *Sinderins* timer/dimmer unit controls the whole arrangement and brings on the main lights during the day if the weather

Outside Roy Aplin's birdroom.

Convention rules in the Aplin birdroom where breeding cages face the inside flights.

becomes dull. Two small electric heaters are controlled by thermostats and two specially-made trays hold water above the heaters to increase the room's humidity. An ioniser helps to keep the air fresh. There is no piped water supply to the room.

Dr Alf Robertson:

My birdroom measures 30ft x 15ft (9.1m x 4.6m) and is brick-built with a concrete floor and tiled roof. Because of the clement climate in Durban, the front wall is "open"; being covered only with wire mesh. The entrance door is towards the right-hand end of one of the long sides and, on entering, there are three tiers of breeding cages on the right-hand end wall and a smaller bank of breeding cages on the facing wall, opposite the door. The centre of the birdroom is taken up by two 15ft x 4ft-6in (4.6m x 1.4m) inside flights. These flights go from wall to wall, so to get into the second large flight, it is necessary to walk through the first. Passing through the second flight brings you to a further three, smaller, interconnected, inside flights (9ft-6in x 3ft-6in (2.9m x 1.1m)) which are used to house young birds and the show team. There is a further bank of breeding cages at this end of the room, separated from the smaller flights by a 9ft-6in (2.9m) long passageway. In total, there are 35 breeding cages; each measuring 32in x 16in x 16in (81cm x 41cm x 41cm). My wooden nest-boxes measure 9in x 6in x 8in (23cm x 15cm x 20cm), are externally mounted and have removable concaves for easy cleaning and replacement. The room's equipments is traditional, consisting of fluorescent lighting to provide the main illumination and low-wattage tungsten bulbs to serve as nightlights. Lighting is controlled by a timer/dimmer unit. To keep the atmosphere even fresher within the room I employ an ioniser and an extractor fan.

Dr. Robertson's birdroom and flights.

A small flight for young Budgerigars, next to the main flight, is used by Alf Robertson.

CHAPTER 2

MANAGEMENT

Describe a typical day's activity in your birdroom during the breeding season:

Eric and Michael Lane:

The first job is to open the flights, so that the birds can go outside. If the weather is going to be warm the windows are opened. Then it is time to check the nest-boxes; eggs laid, chicks hatched, chicks to be ringed. The most important jobs are to make sure that chicks' beaks are not clogged with wet food and that their feet and legs are not coated with droppings. The record book is kept close at hand so that everything is entered and nothing forgotten. It is very easy to forget a ring number or the transfer of eggs or chicks if the information is not written down immediately. Other than giving breeding pairs their softfood, feeding and watering does not take long. The automatic watering system requires virtually no attention and we use large, glass jam jars with hopper bases in the breeding cages and they can last up to two weeks without being refilled. In larger cages we use large pickle jars; the sort you see in fish and chip shops. Once a week, the flights are cleaned out and disinfected; including the perches. Since we have had ceramic-tiled floors throughout the birdroom, including inside the flights, floors are very easy to keep clean.

Jim Hutton:

My main aim, during the breeding season, is to cause as little disturbance as possible so every day, as far as is practicable, I carry out the same duties at the same time in the same way. First job in the morning is to check all cages and flights to make sure all is well. The room's floor is brushed, water dishes checked and softfood given to those pairs that have chicks. They are then left alone until lunchtime. After lunch I make another quick check, particularly of the breeding pairs, to make sure everything is still all right. Now that I have retired I feed the birds around 4pm. All the seed pots are sieved and have the husks blown off. Fresh seed is mixed with the existing to top up the pots. Grit is checked. Water drinkers are washed and clean water given to all cages and flights. Sufficient softfood is made up for two days. Finger drawers are cleaned and filled. Pairs with chicks are given a small dish of bread and milk. (two sets of dishes are used so that one can be washed while the other is in use). The floor is swept and lightly washed with a mop. Only then are nest-boxes checked. Each hen is persuaded to leave its box so that eggs and chicks can be examined. Ringing and transfers are made and a note made on a card that is fixed to the front of the nest-box. The birds are left undisturbed until 9.30pm when a final check is made – particularly of any transferred chicks – the nightlight is switched on and the alarm set for the night. On a weekly basis, dropping trays are removed from cages to be cleaned, an easy job because they are made of glass: a very hygienic arrangement. Seed husks are removed from cage bottoms and nest-boxes containing large chicks have droppings removed and fresh sawdust added. The room's floor is cleaned with disinfectant and the cage fronts are wiped down with a weaker solution of disinfectant. Once a week the information on the nest-box cards is transferred into a ledger.

Roy Aplin:

My first visit to the birdroom takes place early in the morning. Those pairs with chicks are given softfood. I look in the cages to see if any chicks have left the nest too early and – if they have – replace them in the nest-box. I sweep the floor and leave. A more thorough inspection is made in the early evening. Every nest-box is checked and notes are made of eggs laid, chicks hatched and ringed. The health of the parent birds is checked. I like to keep breeding cages as clean as possible and so remove large droppings every day. I do not believe in the deep litter system as it can react like

Roy Aplin uses a 'ladder' in his inside flight to allow moulting Budgerigars to reach the perches.

compost and serve as a breeding ground for bacteria. Coarse sawdust covers the cage floors and there is a board beneath each perch to catch the worst of the droppings. Water is changed every other day and husks are removed from seed dishes, the contents sieved and topped up as necessary. Soiled perches and feeders are replaced by clean ones. I try to space out general cleaning jobs through the week to avoid a build up of work. This gives me time, at the week-ends, to do jobs such as washing down the walls.

Dr Alf Robertson:

I start work in the birdroom at 6 o'clock every morning. Nest-boxes are inspected during this visit and routine, breeding season jobs – such as ringing chicks, cleaning feet and beaks and keeping records up to date – are undertaken. Most of the feeding is also carried out in the morning. Seed and water are topped up or changed and extras, such as soaked oats and softfood, are given. My next main visit is at 5pm. Then, pairs which have chicks are given another supply of soaked oats and softfood. My gardener sweeps out the complete aviary every day and so there is no need to have a special "cleaning day" every week.

Describe the activity in you birdroom during the lead up to a show.

Eric and Michael Lane:

The youngsters are brought in from the flights first; about 6 weeks before the first show. As they are caught, their ring numbers are noted, broken flight and tail feathers are removed and their masks are trimmed to remove excess spots. Then they are sprayed until they are really soaked, with water to which *Johnson's* baby shampoo has been added. This does not sting the birds' eyes. They are then put in groups of six to a 3ft (91cm) long cage. Potential members of the any age show team have their flights and tails checked at the same time – to give them time to grow in again before the show – but they are not caged up or given the rest of the treatment until some three weeks later. After two weeks in stock cages the birds begin to put on a little weight and start to show themselves. The final trimming of masks is done on the Monday before the show. This gives the remaining feathers time to settle back into place. They are sprayed lightly three or four time in the last week, with the final spray being very light indeed. We have show cages fitted to the ends of our stock cages and our birds often go into them to show themselves off. As a consequence they perform very well under show conditions. On the Thursday, all of the show cages are checked over – especially for loose perches. The last job – and one of the most important – is to get the car ready; tyres, petrol, water, all filled up for an early start.

Jim Hutton:

Special attention is given to young birds that show potential. They are taken from the flight and placed in long flight cages. Damaged feathers – except tails – are removed. No matter how much I might want to exhibit a bird, tails are left to moult naturally. In the past there have been occasions when tails have not regrown after being removed. For the first week, to quieten them down, they are confined to half a cage; 10ft (3m) long. After that they are given access to all 20ft (6m). I never have more than eight birds in such a cage, a benefit of keeping a small stud. They are constantly checked and any that are not in the best of condition are returned to the flight. Spraying is always carried out first thing in the morning to permit

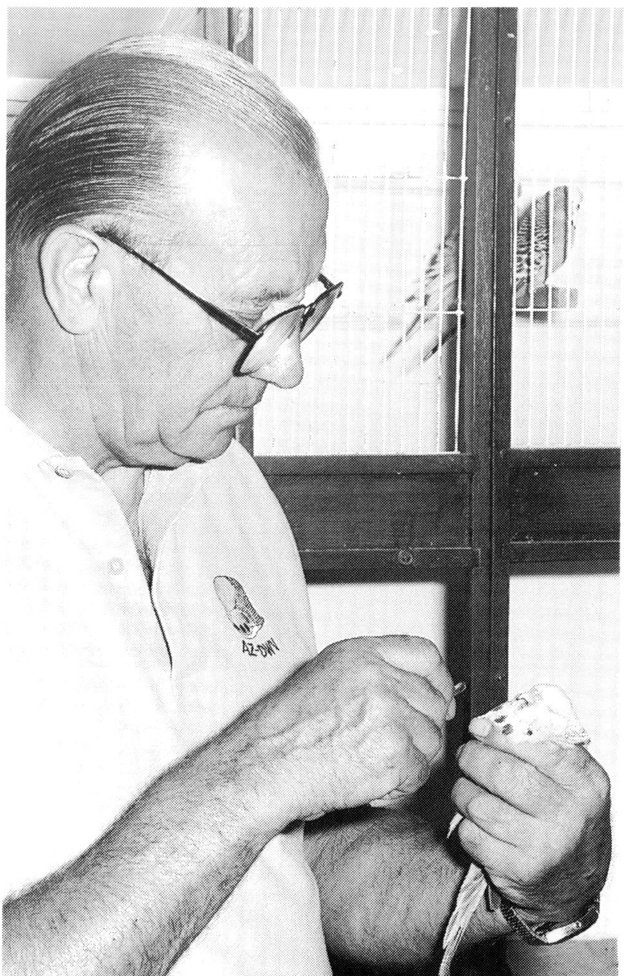

Jim Hutton prepares the mask on this Opaline Cinnamon hen for a show.

plenty of time to dry and masks are trimmed on a progressive basis. I now cut excess mask feathers and this eliminates the problem of unopened spots spoiling masks at later shows. Experience has shown that adult hens are best left in the flight even while they are being sprayed and having their masks trimmed. They hold their condition much longer in a flight. The week before the show is spent making sure that all problems have been dealt with. Reserves are given a last check over in case a last minute disaster stops one of the first-choice show team from being sent. Show cages are cleaned and polished, cage labels are fixed firmly.

Roy Aplin:

About 8 weeks before the first show, a likely show team is caught up. All broken flights and tails are gently removed so that they have time to regrow (we hope!). The show preparation cages are the ones previously used for breeding, but removing dividers creates cages that are two, three or four units long. The size of the cage a particular bird is kept in is determined by its weight. It is important to have enough weight on a show Budgerigar – but not too much. I like my show team to be housed in very clean cages with very clean perches. Pink mineral blocks are removed so that faces do not become discoloured. Spraying depends a great deal on each bird's feather condition. Budgerigars that are 100 per cent fit do not need spraying. For others, spraying (with rainwater) starts about six weeks before the show and

Roy Aplin keeps his show team in clean cages with clean perches.

continues until halfway through the last week. Also in the last week, tails and the head feathering above the cere are hand-washed with lukewarm water and liquid soap. If a blood quill breaks on a Budgerigar's head you can try washing with saltwater, milk or cold water – but in my experience the operation is never entirely successful. De-spotting is often left until the day before the show. Some may think this a little late but, in the past, I have known birds to drop spots just after their masks have been trimmed. I find that cutting the excess spots gives a neater finish than pulling them – and is much kinder to the birds. I believe that immaculate show cages complement the birds they contain, so I start preparing them a week before the show in case paintwork needs touching up. It is important that Budgerigars are well fed before going to a show so I add millet sprays, dry oats and groats to their diet during the last few hours. For transportation to shows, the show cages are put into carrying boxes. This limits the disturbance the Budgerigars experience. I prefer one-day shows which permit my birds to spend the night before and the night after in my own birdroom. However, to compete fully, it is necessary to enter longer shows – such as the Budgerigar Society Club Show. At two-day shows, after judging I give my Budgerigars millet sprays that have been soaked in a solution of *Vanodine V18* to persuade them to eat. On arrival home, my show birds are kept in stock cages for two days to feed them up and help them recover from their outing.

Dr Alf Robertson:

When I select the show team, I make sure that there are plenty of reserves. The team is housed in double-breeder cages with double-sized training show cages attached to their ends. The main tail feathers are gently removed eight weeks before the first show and mask spots are removed five weeks before the show. The weights of the show candidates are assessed and those that need a little extra weight have soaked oats added to their basic diet. Care is taken not to let any bird that is overweight have access to the oats. Spraying begins as soon as the show team is caught up and continues on a daily basis until three days before the show. During the week leading up to the show, every member of the show team is placed in an individual show cage. They stay in these all night and are returned to the double-breeder cages when I make my morning visit to the birdroom. The spots in the newly-grown masks are trimmed four days before the show.

CHAPTER 3

FEEDING

How do you feed your Budgerigars?

Eric and Michael Lane:

<u>**Basic seed mixture:**</u>

Our basic seed mixture is *Trill*. We have used *Trill* for many years and find it to be an excellent seed mixture.

A feeding station like this is used in all Eric Lane's breeding cages.

Extras:

Trill softfood is fed twice a week in small pots or finger drawers. All the year round, all stock – except the show team in the few weeks prior to a show – is given sliced carrot twice a week. *Harker's Hormova* is sprinkled on top of the seed in the open dishes in the flights and *Harker's Hormoform* is fed in finger drawers to breeding pairs. Greenfood is never fed. All pairs with youngsters are given a cube of white bread damped with milk, every day. When there are youngsters in nest-boxes and cages we use lots of millet sprays.

Drinking water:

Our automatic watering system works off the mains but the water passes through two filters before the birds drink it. It is an excellent system that has never caused problems. We drain and clean it every two or three weeks.

Additives:

Harker's Budgerigar Tonic is given in the drinking water once a year – usually after the birds have been on a course of *Trykil* (see chapter 4). The tonic is given in water fountains. If it was done via the automatic watering system it would take a great deal of the additive. The best – and easiest – time is just before breeding, when numbers are at their lowest and most of the birds are in the flights.

Grit and minerals:

Each cage is equipped with a small pot of mineral grit with a little charcoal added. This pot is topped up every week. Each cage has a piece of cuttlefish bone fixed firmly to the cage front. This is checked regularly and replaced as necessary. The breeding season starts with new iodine nibbles fixed to every cage.

Jim Hutton:

Basic seed mixture:

My basic seed mixture varies according to the time of the year. During the breeding season, Budgerigars need high protein seed, preferably with a soft kernel – such as English-grown canary seed; naturally harvested and dried without artificial heat. I have known plain canary seed, imported from Europe, to be anything up to five years old, dried out and lacking in protein. For the breeding season each cage has three seed dishes. The largest has 75 per cent English canary and 25 per cent Canadian canary. The second pot has *Haith's* Budgerigar tonic seed with added groats and a small amount of sunflower seeds. The third pot contains mixed millets; 50 per cent Japanese, 25 per cent white and 25 per cent red. Thus a varied diet is offered and it is surprising how a pair's consumption of different seeds varies at different stages of their chicks' development. Experience has shown that the pairs which take mainly canary seed usually have the biggest and best youngsters. In the non-breeding season the English canary seed is removed from the diet. The soft kernel – so beneficial in the breeding season – works against getting Budgerigars into tight-feather condition needed for shows. I learnt this lesson when I exhibited English Game Bantams. The driest and hardest wheat available was needed to get them into show condition. It is the same with Budgerigars and I feed *Trill* to keep my birds in good feather condition.

Extras:

Extras are generally for the breeding season. I make a dry-mix at the start of the breeding season and store it in plastic containers. My mix consists of *Maxi-feed*, *EMP*, dried milk, powdered egg, soya flour, glucose, dried meat and bone plus a German-made egg and vitamin supplement made by *Quiko*, in Germany. When the time comes to feed, I finely chop a hardboiled egg, add a teaspoonful of honey and a few drops of cod liver oil. This is beaten together and used to moisten the softfood mixture to a crumbly consistency. This is fed in finger drawers; twice a day to pairs with chicks and once to those without. A small cube of bread, damped with milk, is also given to feeding pairs. Chickweed, which grows in abundance in my garden, is fed twice a week from November to April in very small amounts – except if there is any frost around. Weaned chicks have the same diet as the rest of the birds with the addition of an occasional millet spray. If too many millet sprays are offered, youngsters may refuse to eat anything else. I am fortunate to be able to obtain a supply of small red millet sprays, grown in Germany. These are rich in protein and iron and much appreciated by my birds.

Drinking water:

Drinking water has caused the death of many Budgerigars. Tap water is full of chlorine and other chemicals and is never consistent. I collect rainwater from the extension to my house, which is free of wild bird droppings. It is collected in a large plastic container to which has been added *Vanodine V18*.

Additives:

About a month before the breeding season I add *Solvit* to the drinking water at half the recommended strength (5ml to a 1.7pt (1l) of water).

Grit and minerals:

Grit is important to the general health of birds so I choose the best grits available; a mixture of small limestone and oystershell. This is available at all times in the flight, offered in a hopper so that it is always clean. I use grit and mineral cones made by *Alfred Merkl*, in Nurnberg, Germany – but now available in the UK. These contain various minerals and grit collected from mountain streams and have all the necessary trace elements that are not available in seed alone. Cuttlefish bone is a must – and always available.

Roy Aplin:

Basic seed mixture:

The basic diet is *Trill*; a good all-round seed which my Budgerigars like and so there is no waste. In the lead-up to the breeding season a little Budgerigar tonic seed is fed. During the breeding season, those pairs that consume the plain canary quickly have the proportion of this seed increased. Occasionally, small sunflower seeds are added to the mixture.

Extras:

Those pairs that will eat it are given wholemeal bread and milk until their chicks are 10 days old. There is a very wide choice of proprietary softfood and I have tried a lot of them. At present I make a mixture of *EMP*, *Trill* softfood, hard-boiled eggs and grated carrots. Soaked oats are fed in moderation, with care being taken to look out for hens that become messy feeders and clog up chicks' beaks. Sprouting mung beans are fed as are chickweed and seeding grasses, when available. Millet sprays are fed all the year around but in the breeding season they are cut into short lengths and put into nest-boxes containing chicks that are four weeks and older. It tempts chicks to begin feeding themselves and prevents hens from becoming bored - or even aggressive. A recent addition to my birds' diet are red millet sprays from Germany. British Budgerigars benefit greatly from these and I have successfully grown my own.

Drinking water:

In the past, I have used rainwater but became worried about pollution in the atmosphere. I have tried boiling water and filtering water, but now my birds' drinking water just comes straight from the tap. Although my normal practice is to change the drinking water every other day, in very hot weather I change it every day.

Additives:

Additives tend to be a matter of fashion. We hear that someone is having a super breeding season and we hope to emulate him by using the same products that he claims are responsible for his success. When it doesn't work we try another. The problem is that different breeders have different feeding programmes and so an additive that is just right for one might be no use at all to another. In the past I have used *Abidec*, *Cytacon* and vitamin B in the drinking water, but I am going through a "basic feeding" phase. But, who knows, next season I could be using an additive that someone has convinced me is a wonder product.

Grit and minerals:

I use a wide variety of grits; *Versel-laga*, *Caperns*, extra oyster shell and added charcoal. I give my birds mineral block that come from Germany and they enjoy them. In the breeding and stock cages I use white *Liverine* mineral blocks (they seem to last longer than the pink ones) and in the flights I use *Liverine* Pigeon blocks. Cuttlefish bone is offered when available and mortar from old buildings. *Kilpatricks*' Pigeon minerals and pink Pigeon minerals complete this section.

Dr Alf Robertson:

Basic seed mixture:

My Budgerigars' basic seed mixture consists of a 50/50 mix of white millet and Japanese millet. They receive NO plain canary seed. I realise that is contrary to the approach of the vast majority of Budgerigar breeders, but it works for me. My Budgerigars are fit, healthy and breed as well as any that eat canary seed. This could be because as a daily, supplementary seed mixture I feed pearl millet, sunflower seed, buckwheat and mixed Sudan grass seeds.

Extras:

In the breeding season - and when I want to put weight on a bird - I feed soaked oats. My softfood mixture consists of brown breadcrumbs, milk, raw egg and sugar mixed to a semi-dry consistency. Greenfood is fed only very occasionally.

Drinking water:

My Budgerigars receive tap water, with a vitamin supplement added three times a week.

Additives:

I use a water-soluble multi-vitamin supplement, as mentioned above.

Grit and minerals:

Grit is supplied to the breeding cages but not to the flights. The breeding pairs also receive home-made balls of plaster of Paris (calcium carbonate). Cuttlefish bone is always available.

CHAPTER 4

MEDICATION

What do you look for when checking your birds' health and what do you do about it?

Eric and Michael Lane:

If we see any birds with dull eyes, clogged vents or sitting fluffed up, we know they are under the weather and so cage them up and bring them into the house to be kept warm. Another sign to look for is the bird that sits in the same place for long periods. This could be a symptom of illness. Birds with clogged vents have the droppings gently removed and their vents are washed with a solution of *Dettol.* They are then caged so that we can keep an eye on them. As well as keeping them warm, any birds showing the symptoms described are put on a course of terramycin in their drinking water – as supplied and advised by a vet.

Jim Hutton:

It is not always easy to tell when a bird is not well but experience gives you an intuition. Illness is easier to treat if you catch it early. By the time a vent is clogged (clagging) it could be too late. The most common illness, at the moment, is thrush, the symptom of which is a dampness around the face; as though the bird has rubbed its head in water. It is easily cured by isolating the bird and treating with two drops of *Nystan.* This is usually effective, but if the bird does not respond a further two drops are given. If that does not work a 7 day course of terramycin usually effects a cure. If not treated, thrush develops to a build-up of mucous around the beak and ultimately to entiritis, which is nearly impossible to cure. Diarrhoea and clagging are the other main ailments and, again, easily cured if caught quickly. My treatment is two drops of a diarrhoea mixture into the beak followed by three days on *Entrodex* probiotic. I do not use a hospital cage as I believe this dehydrates the patient.

Roy Aplin:

As long as you have livestock there will always be a risk of encountering health problems. Stock must be checked carefully every day. Young birds, after first being released into the flight are particularly vulnerable and need extra attention. They (particularly the better ones) can soon lose weight and become green around the vent. They should be caught up immediately and put into cages; their vents washed and millet sprays provided to tempt them to eat. If you do not keep vents clean, the birds will do it themselves and so recycle an illness through their systems – which must be a bad thing. Cold tea can be effective for stomach upsets.

Dr Alf Robertson:

I am always looking out for any bird that is fluffed up, has a wet vent or a clogged vent. Any bird showing such signs is isolated and treated with appropriate medication.

What does your birdroom's medicine chest contain?

Eric and Michael Lane:

Terramycin; *Trykil* (Emtryl soluble); *Vanodine V18* and *Domestos* bleach (as disinfectants); eye ointment, *Johnson's Anti-peck* and *Nivea* cream (against feather plucking); cotton wool buds, scaly-face cream and *Ivomec* (in case of scaly-face); clear iodine (for any skin abrasions); *Johnson's Baby Shampoo*, glycerine and *Plume-spray* (for show preparation).

Jim Hutton:

Nystan, *Entrodex*, a diarrhoea mixture, *Trykil* (to prevent trichomoniasis) and *Ivomec* (for scaly face, but hardly ever required).

Roy Aplin:

Trykil, *Nilverm*, terramycin, glycerine and surgical spirit (for birds – mainly hens – that have skin irritation around the neck; curable if treated early), eye drops for conjunctivitis (veterinary type, as prescribed for cats and dogs), *Duramitex* (for washing equipment and to prevent mite infestations), witch hazel (for stiff claws and swollen legs), *Vanodine V18* (disinfectant), benzyl benzoate as a treatment for scaly-face.

Dr Alf Robertson:

Terramycin, *Tricho-plus*, *Maxitral* eye ointment.

Do you use medication on a routine, preventative basis?

Eric and Michael Lane:

Trykil (Emtryl soluble) is used routinely against trichomoniasis every October. The recommended one week course is administered followed by a tonic. In the distant past, antibiotics and de-wormers were used but no other routine medication is now administered.

Jim Hutton:

Trikyl (Emtryl soluble) is administered twice a year; before and after the breeding season. Antibiotics are given only to individuals and only when required.

Roy Aplin:

Cleanliness and a good diet are the best preventatives against illness. Overcrowding can cause illness to break out and any new bird should be isolated for five to six weeks before being integrated into the stud. I de-worm my Budgerigars once a year with *Nilverm.* Today's large Budgerigars are susceptible to worms and definitely need to be treated. A course of *Trykil* (Emtryl soluble) is given before the breeding season as a preventative against trichomoniasis. Antibiotics are given only when required – and even then in moderation.

Dr Alf Robertson:

My stock is treated twice a year with *Tricho-plus* (a medicine to treat trichomoniasis) and terramycin antibiotic.

CHAPTER 5

THEIR STUDS

(Readers who are not conversant with the genetics of colour expectation will find it helpful to refer to Chapter 7 when the experts discuss pairings that produce Opalines and Opaline Cinnamons).

How many Budgerigars do you keep and what varieties are they?

Eric and Michael Lane:

We keep around 200 Budgerigars from which we choose 60 breeding pairs. About two-thirds of our Budgerigars, around 140, are Opalines and Opaline Cinnamons. The remainder are made up of Normal Greens, Blues, Greys and Grey Greens, Dominant Pieds in their Normal and Opaline forms, Yellowfaces and Spangles. We also keep a few Albinos, a part of our stud which is coming along very nicely.

Jim Hutton:

At the start of the breeding season I usually have 12 good cock birds and around 16 hens; some of which are late bred and flown over to the following season. Ideally, six of the cocks will be Opaline Cinnamon or split for Opaline Cinnamon and around 10 Opaline Cinnamon hens. This is not easy to achieve because culling is done only on the basis of quality; not on colour or variety. I prefer Grey Greens to Light Greens but if the quality of the latter is very good I have to retain more. I retain a few Normals (usually Greys or Grey Greens) to pair back to my Opaline Cinnamons as I feel that this helps both varieties. I also have a few Spangles which, when paired with Normals, produce first-class Spangles and Normals. Occasionally an odd Cinnamon Spangle hen crops up and the quality is invariably outstanding. I tend to pair these with good Cinnamon cocks and retain the Normal Cinnamons produced. I dispose of the Cinnamon Spangles because I want, as much as possible, to keep only Normal Spangles. In my view, crossing Spangles with too many other varieties has been responsible for them losing the definition of the their markings.

Roy Aplin:

Just prior to the breeding season I have around 150 Budgerigars. I always keep a high proportion of hens because it is among these that most breeding season problems are encountered. For a few outstanding cock birds

I reserve three special hens each. I like both Normals and Opalines but the latter have always been the backbone of my stud and so approximately half of my birds are Opalines or Opaline Cinnamons. I keep Normal Greys, Grey Greens, Skyblues, Cinnamons, Spangles and a few Light Greens.

Dr Alf Robertson:

I usually keep around 300 Budgerigars and, of these, about 120 are Opalines and Opaline Cinnamons. The rest is made up of Normals, Spangles, Cinnamons and Lacewings.

Which of the other varieties can improve your Opalines and Opaline Cinnamons?

Eric and Michael Lane:

Generally speaking, we do not cross other varieties into our Opaline line. Opaline to Opaline has proved to be very successful in the past as it helps to keep clean heads and clean backs. Having said that, the Opaline that everyone remembers displayed flecking; the one that won at the BS Club Show three years running, plus best in show at the National Exhibition and Budgerigar World. He looked at his very best at the BS Convention in 1990, where some visitors said he was the best Budgerigar they had ever seen. Big, flecked Opalines can be very important in the breeding cage; they have so many desirable features – but it does take time to get to a stage where you are producing young Opalines without flecking. However, to be worth using in the breeding team a flecked Budgerigar must be absolutely outstanding. On the other hand, we have found Normal Cinnamons to be useful in the production of high-quality Opaline Cinnamons. Many of our pairings are Opaline Cinnamon x Normal Cinnamon.

Jim Hutton:

It depends entirely upon what features you are trying to improve. For example, the Yellowface mutation crossed into my Opaline Cinnamon Grey Greens gives a beautiful mustard colour which virtually shines. But there is no point in improving body colour if the rest of the bird is inferior. Only the very best Yellowfaces are good enough to cross into my Opaline Cinnamons. If ever I feel that my Opaline Cinnamons are losing body size or feather length I dip into my Normals. Any Budgerigar you introduce into a line must have something to offer; depth of mask, larger spots, backskull, deportment, etc. It all depends which features you wish to improve.

Roy Aplin:

Some of my best Opaline Cinnamons have been bred from Opaline Grey Green/Cinnamon cocks. Some breeders say that pairing Opaline Cinnamon WITH Opaline Cinnamon reduces the size of the youngsters, but many of my Opaline Cinnamon winners have been bred this way. I have always tried to achieve rich coloration in my Opaline Cinnamon Grey Greens and a good way, I found, is to pair an Opaline Yellow cock with an Opaline Cinnamon Grey Green hen. Although this does not produce any Opaline Cinnamons in the first generation, the young Opaline cocks are split for Cinnamon and so are quite capable of producing Opaline Cinnamons themselves. Over the years, Normal and Opaline Grey Greens have been very strong varieties that are quite capable of improving virtually any other.

Dr Alf Robertson:

Most of my Normal Grey Greens are split Opaline and, over the years, the Grey Greens have helped to improve the Opalines and the Opalines have helped to improve the Grey Greens. A big problem with Opalines is their tendency to get short in the face and deep-faced Normals are ideal for maintaining and improving the faces of Opalines.

(above) Dr. Robertson's garden and outside flight in Durban, South Africa.

(right) A super Grey Green cock bred by Dr. Robertson from an Opaline hen and a split Opaline cock.

(above) Roy Aplin spraying a Budgerigar in a show cage.

(left) In the Aplin birdroom, good use is made of space. These cages which are at the end of the room, are shaped to admit light into the breeding units on the back wall of his birdroom. (photographs: Les Lockey)

A big winner for Eric and Michael Lane! This Opaline Grey Green cock has taken many challenge certificates for the partnership. (photograph: Les Lockey)

(above) Jim Hutton's birdroom. Flights and breeding room are one unit.

(left) Nest-box inspection time for Jim Hutton. (photographs: Les Lockey)

Opaline Cinnamon Grey Green hen bred by Jim Hutton.(photograph: Les Lockey)

(above) *It's the breeding season in Eric Lane's birdroom.*

(left) *Opaline Cinnamon cock from the Lane & Son's stud. (photographs: Les Lockey)*

Opaline Light Green cock – Lane & Son. (photograph: Les Lockey)

(right) Opaline Cinnamon Grey Green cock – Roy Aplin.

(left) A deep-faced Opaline Cobalt cock – Lane & Son.
(photographs: Les Lockey)

(left) Opaline Grey cock – Jim Hutton.

(right) Another top quality Opaline Grey Green cock produced by Eric and Michael Lane. (photographs: Les Lockey)

Opaline Grey cock – Roy Aplin. (photograph: Les Lockey)

This Opaline Skyblue cock bred by Roy Aplin, although slightly flecked, is ideal for the breeding cage.(photograph: Les Lockey)

Opaline Cinnamon Skyblue cock – Jim Hutton.
(photograph: Les Lockey)

CHAPTER 6

ALL ABOUT OPALINES AND OPALINE CINNAMONS

What is the attraction of Opalines and Opaline Cinnamons and is specialising a good idea?

Eric and Michael Lane:

I was attracted to Opalines from the first time I saw them. My father built Harry Bryan's cages, when he lived at Sutton Coldfield, and I went along to help. I couldn't take my eyes off the lovely, brightly-coloured, clean Opalines and asked Mr Bryan if he would sell me a pair of Opaline Greens. He said that a young Opaline Skyblue cock would be best and I bought him – along with an Opaline Skyblue hen, an Opaline Dark Green cock with an undershot beak and a Yellowface Opaline Grey hen. These were the first birds I ever bought and buying them from Harry Bryan I was starting with the best. A few months later I exhibited the young Opaline Skyblue cock at the BS Club Show – on the only occasion it was staged at Birmingham's Bingley Hall. It came third in the any age class, behind two Bryan Opalines. The class winner (the father of my young cock) went on to be best in show. Opalines are more difficult to breed to a constant high standard than Normals. They have more features that can be faulted; heads should be clear, backs should be clean and wings should not be patchy – all those in addition to the problems faced by Normal breeders. This is part of the challenge for us. We have won nearly everything that can be won but winning still brings a buzz of excitement. Although I love Opalines and Opaline Cinnamons we have always kept a range of colours but there is no doubt that you tend to favour the varieties that you do best with. We have had luck with Opalines and Opaline Cinnamons and so have a reputation for specialising in them.

Jim Hutton:

When my father started to keep exhibition Budgerigars, in 1936, he was very successful. At the start of World War II he was taking best in show awards at some of Scotland's largest shows. He bought birds from many sources but one I remember particularly was a Cinnamon cock from

Frank Waite. It was the loveliest bird I had ever seen. Unfortunately the stud was sold in 1942 and I started again from scratch after my army service. It was 1950 by the time I was ready to buy birds and I chose the name of P.G. Perry, of Wakefield in Yorkshire, from an advertisement in *CAGE & AVIARY BIRDS*. He let me have two pairs at a reasonable price, one of which was a pair of Cinnamons. From these I bred Opaline Cinnamon hens and a Cinnamon Cobalt cock which did well on the show bench. I was hooked! I still think that Opaline Cinnamons, with their brown markings and soft, dilute colouring, are the most attractive of all Budgerigars. I have achieved a great deal on the show bench with Opaline Cinnamons but I still set myself the task of breeding a real wonder bird each year. The last time I achieved it was in 1990, with an Opaline Cinnamon Blue hen. Since then there have been outstanding Grey Greens and Spangles. I feel that the best of the progeny of the 1990 hen have still to be seen. I believe it is essential to specialise or you would finish up with a hotch-potch of colours. By specialising in a variety that is not as popular as Normals you find it easier to acquire good stock.

Roy Aplin:

In the 1960s, when I set up my present stud, Opalines were dominating the scene and I felt that I had little choice when I set out to buy Budgerigars on which a successful stud could be based. The late Charles Hayter was primarily a breeder of Lutinos but he also kept some very good Opalines. I was very lucky to purchase two Budgerigars from him that were only a few weeks old; an Opaline Skyblue cock and an Opaline Cinnamon Skyblue hen. About the same time I acquired an Opaline Grey, which was related to the Hayter birds, from Jim Godsell. Combining these birds in the breeding programme produced Budgerigars that scored some very surprising wins on the show bench. I then realsised that I had, in fact, started a little way up the ladder, rather than at the bottom. I soon developed the Opaline Cinnamons for which I have become known, but even after 20 years, I still feel that it is a great achievement to win a challenge certificate for the variety. To win a higher award is an even greater achievement because Opalines and Opaline Cinnamons have fallen behind Normals in recent years. Whether to specialise or not is up to the individual breeder. Even when a fancier sets out to specialise in one variety they often have to introduce other varieties to bring about improvements. In the end it is the overall quality of a Budgerigar that matters most, not whether it is one variety or another.

Dr Alf Robertson:

I started with Opalines by accident in 1955, when I bought a Normal cock from Ken Farmer, one of the leading UK Budgerigar breeders. It turned out to be split Opaline and bred some very nice Opalines for me.

Later, I acquired several Maurice Finey-bred birds from Brian Byles and these strengthened the stud considerably. I was attracted to Opalines by their typically-good exhibition features: excellent size, bold heads and large mask spots – and it is these same features that encourage me to carry on keeping them. In my opinion, any good Normal stud needs Opalines and a good Opaline stud needs Normals. I think that specialising in Opalines is a good idea because, unless you have a very large stud indeed, you cannot do justice to a large number of varieties. If you want to do well, consistently, with a particular variety, you need to specialise.

What makes a good – and a bad – Opaline or Opaline Cinnamon?

Eric and Michael Lane:

When I was learning about Budgerigars, Harry Bryan used to tell me that to be a good one, a Budgerigar does not have to be big and ugly; what is sometimes called a "power bird". He explained that a Budgerigar

An Opaline Cinnamon hen from the Hutton stud – a good one!

that is well-balanced, has good colour and holds its tail well is always in with a chance of winning. An outstanding Opaline or Opaline Cinnamon should have a nice width of head, plenty of height above the eye, a clean frontal and back, a punched-in face (like a boxer dog), a deep, wide mask with large well-shaped spots, well-defined wing markings and stand up well to show itself off when put in a show cage. Bad faults are: narrow head, flat head, short mask, small spots, lack of size, hinged or dropped tail, dropped wings, flecked heads, washed out or patchy body colour, dirty back and wing markings that look as if they have been smudged.

Jim Hutton:

A good Budgerigar is a good Budgerigar regardless of its colour, so the description of a high-quality bird will apply to any variety. First, it must have good deportment; sitting at the proper angle of 30 deg to the vertical. It must have good, wide shoulders, a good width of head with adequate backskull, an excellent depth of mask (with no division) with large round spots that are evenly spaced and not overlapping. The tail must be in line with the back and the wing flights must tuck neatly at the rump. The overall length should not be less than $8\frac{1}{2}$ in (22cm). It is essential for a Budgerigar to look in proportion. There are numerous faults, the most serious of which is a dropped tail. Other bad faults are narrow head, narrow shoulders, short mask, small spots, crossed wings carried high above the rump and a large, protruding beak.

Roy Aplin:

If you study the winners of the Opaline and Opaline Cinnamon classes at a championship show, you will have some idea of what makes a good specimen. It takes years of experience to appreciate the very fine points that make the difference between a good one and one that is almost good. A bad Opaline or Opaline Cinnamon is one that is very small, very fine feathered, narrow between the eyes, short in the mask, beaky, has crossed or dropped wings, a hinged tail and poor deportment. In fact, a Budgerigar that would make a good pet – and nothing else!

Dr Alf Robertson:

A good Opaline – obviously – is one that conforms to the Ideal for the variety. However, to explain a little more, an Opaline with a large, clear yellow or white face, cap and clear, body-coloured saddle combined with a deep mask that carries large, deeply-spaced spots certainly makes everyone stop and look. Which makes it pretty obvious what features make a bad one:

not conforming to the Ideal, having head flecking, a dirty back and a short mask.

Which faults are correctable and which are not?

Eric and Michael Lane:

The hardest faults to correct are narrow head, short mask, dropped tail and dropped wings. We would not breed from Budgerigars that have these faults. Poor body colour can be corrected by pairing with Dark factor birds (Dark Green, Olive, Cobalt, Violet or Mauve) or pairing to Normal. Some breeders advise against pairing Opaline with Opaline, but we do it and I am convinced that is why we breed so many with clean heads and backs. Flecked Opaline hens can also be paired with Normal cocks to breed unflecked Normals. Opaline Grey hens, no matter how heavily flecked, make very good mates for Albino cocks. Trying to breed with Budgerigars with the other faults listed is more trouble than it is worth.

Jim Hutton:

Dropped tails are virtually impossible to breed out, as are crossed wings – though we see very little of the latter fault, these days. The other faults I have listed are bad, but they can be bred out by careful selective breeding. However, if one bird has several faults it is best to forget about breeding from it. The potential for breeding out faults depends upon what stock you have available and not everyone has a super stud to work with. In the final analysis you can only use the birds that are available to you so the main principle to work to is that it is always inadvisable to pair together two Budgerigars that have the same fault. Where possible, I try to pair together birds which complement each other. I rarely use a Budgerigar in the breeding team that is lacking in width of both face and shoulder. Lack of deportment is a fault that can make an otherwise good Budgerigar into a loser. The breeders who concentrate on fixing good deportment in their studs are the ones who enjoy most success on the show bench. First impressions are usually right – and that goes for Budgerigar judges, too. A Budgerigar that displays a lot of swank MUST command a judge's attention.

Roy Aplin:

Most faults are correctable – given sufficient time. Hinged tail, for example, would take an extremely long time to breed out. If I had a large Budgerigar with a massive head and excellent in every other respect –

except that it dropped its tail – I would be prepared to work with the bird to try to breed out the fault. It would be a matter of finding mates that did not have any signs of dropped tail in its pedigree for many generations. In real life you have to make the best use of the birds you have at your disposal, by balancing their good and bad features. To go out and buy a new Budgerigar every time you detected a slight fault would be impossible. Even if it was possible it would take a lot of money. With Opalines and Opaline Cinnamons, you have the added problem of marking faults – eg: dirty back and head flecking – on an otherwise good Budgerigar.

Dr Alf Robertson:

When dealing with a specific mutation, it is the particular characteristics of the variety that have to be considered. With Opalines, this means the markings. In my years of breeding Opalines, I have not found a way of curing dirty backs. By contrast, I DID find a way of getting rid of head flecking. At one time my primary use for flecked Opalines was to improve my Normals. Then, I began pairing flecked Opaline with flecked Opaline and, after several generations, the flecking decreased.

Plenty of top quality youngsters from the Lane stud have passed through these baby cages.

What do you see as being the strength of your own stud? What do you think of other breeders' and other countries' Opalines and Opaline Cinnamons?

Eric and Michael Lane:

We believe that the strength of our stud, at the moment, lies in its Opalines, Opaline Cinnamons and Normal Cinnamons. At the 1993 BS Club Show we had four first prizes, three with Opalines as well as many seconds and thirds. We took the Cinnamon young bird challenge certificate with a cock that was bred from an Opaline Cinnamon hen. Although we are satisfied with the size of the majority of our Budgerigars, we would still like to put on a little more feathering. Perhaps the best young Budgerigar I saw in 1993 was Winsper & Fish's Opaline Light Green hen. As well as being massive it was a wonderful show bird, you would have great difficulty in faulting her. I visited the aviaries of Gren and Pat Norris, before they had their best birds stolen, and was very impressed with the quality of their stock. They have great potential for breeding top-quality Dark-factor Budgerigars. I also saw two outstanding studs of exhibition Budgerigars when I visited Cornish fanciers, Rodney Harris and Arthur Piper. As far as overseas is concerned, I saw one or two promising Opalines when I was in the USA in 1990. Jeff Watkins' and John Miller's Opaline Skyblues were excellent, having taken several best in shows. While judging in Germany, Switzerland, Italy and Jersey I have seen nice Opalines in every country. At the Swiss Budgerigar Club Show an Opaline Cinnamon was best in show. Overall, one man stands head and shoulders above everyone else as a Budgerigar breeder. He is Harry Bryan. I remember him visiting my father and me and advising us to pair a big-spotted Opaline Cobalt cock to an Opaline Violet hen which we didn't rate at all. They produced 11 chicks and every one won on the show bench. One Opaline Skyblue cock took best in show awards many times. When Harry's Opaline Grey Green cock (a real cracker) was best in show at the BS Club Show, he offered us one of its sisters; an Opaline Light Green hen. We paired her with an Opaline Cinnamon Grey Green cock and bred the Opaline Grey Green cock that was best breeder at the BS Club Show in 1974 and best Opaline in show for three years running. This was the good line that bred our Opaline Cinnamons; with beautifully clean heads and backs. The Grey Greens were a lovely mustard colour. We must mention Alf Ormerod. He was a great breeder of good Budgerigars. I once awarded the Cinnamon and Dominant Pied challenge certificates to his birds at London & Southern Counties area championships. They were great big Budgerigars and one took best in show and the other was second best. I always liked Smith & Wainwright's Opaline Cinnamons. Vic and Stan had some great birds which always did well at the BS Club Show. Jack Fisher's superb Grey cock was the biggest Budgerigar I have ever seen. It well deserved its best breeder in show award at the BS Club Show. It was a sad loss to the Fancy when Jack passed away.

Jim Hutton:

The strength of my stud is its ability to produce good hens, year after year. My hardest task now is deciding which to keep and which to let go. I am now disposing of hens which, a few years ago, I would have retained. However, being able to let good birds go makes it easier to arrange an exchange. My father once said that I was never satisfied with my own birds. That is still true today and I am forever trying to improve them. Even when I breed a super bird I can see where it could be improved. That is one reason I seldom retain a bird for more than two breeding seasons; even ones that win best in show. The improvement I am working on at the moment is to have the head feathers on each side of the cere growing outwards to give the appearance of more width. I always admire the good Budgerigars produced by other breeders but there are few fanciers in Britain with studs that have strength in depth. Many have an isolated, excellent bird and this takes them to the top for a short period – and then they are gone. Fanciers who have the type of Budgerigars I like are Jim Moffat, Chris Snell (who produced them with his late father, Arthur) and Rodney Harris. They all have feather quality and type in their birds. However, the person with the most outstanding stud of Budgerigars is Jo Mannes of Freiburg. His stud has to be seen to be believed, excelling in virtually every desirable feature: feather,

This example of an Opaline Cinnamon Light Green cock shows the strength of Roy Aplin's stock.

head, mask, spots and, most important, deportment. In my view there is no stud in Britain that compares with that of Jo Mannes. Having said that, the quality of Opaline Cinnamons in continental Europe does not compare with Britain. I have judged many shows in Germany and so have seen most of the top birds. Jo Mannes has the odd good Opaline Cinnamon but they are not as good as his Normal Cinnamons. There have been many good Opaline Cinnamons in the past. Smith & Wainwright had many excellent examples in the early 1960s, the only problem was that they were the forerunners of flecked Budgerigars. Mrs Angela Moss had some really outstanding Opaline Cinnamon Grey Green cocks in the 1960s. These were the best ever bred and would still be winning today. I remember Harry Bryan taking the top award at the Midland Budgerigar Association, best breeder at the Budgerigar Society Club Show and best in show the following year with super Opaline Cinnamons. More recently, Eric and Michael Lane had good Opaline Cinnamons, one of which took best in show at Budgerigar World, two years running. All were top breeders of their time and I think their winners would beat the Opaline Cinnamons that are winning today.

Roy Aplin:

As they have proved so many times, Opaline Cinnamons are the strength of my stud, particularly Opaline Cinnamon Grey Greens. I have had the opportunity to spend a lot of time with Harry Bryan since he came to live in the south of England and he has always drummed into me that style and deportment are essential in exhibition Budgerigars. I believe I have fixed these features in my stud but I am always working at maintaining and improving head quality and depth of mask. As far as Opaline Cinnamons are concerned, Lane & Son have had wonderful specimens over the years. There are so many other excellent studs that this book would not be long enough to mention them all, however, when considering quality Budgerigars rather than particular colours, the studs of Jo Mannes in Germany and Jorge De Pina in Brazil are outstanding. I have judged in several countries and on the basis of what I have seen I would say that Britain still leads the way with Opaline Cinnamons, but the Opalines in Germany would take some beating. Comparing today's best Budgerigars with those of the past, my conclusion is that modern Budgerigars have far more feather, bigger heads, deeper masks and wider shoulders. I would not say that today's Budgerigars are bigger. In fact many of them appear to be shorter because of the increased emphasis on head size. Taking all factors into account I believe that Budgerigars are better now than they have ever been. In the 1960s, when I started seriously, it was almost like a closed shop with people like Harry Bryan, Angela Moss, Ken Farmer, Lane & Son, Alf Ormerod and Tom Rothery winning everything. In those days I remember shows where all the challenge certificates went to champion exhibits. These days the good Budgerigars are much more evenly spread and it is normal to see challenge certificates being taken by beginners.

Dr Alf Robertson:

The strength of my own stud is the way that the Opalines and Normals it contains blend so well together. The Normal split Opaline cocks produce wonderful Opaline hens. I would still like to make further improvements on such features as depth of mask, rise and width on the head frontal, capping over and in front of the eyes and feather quality. I greatly admire what Jo Mannes, of Germany, has achieved with exhibition Budgerigars. He has an insight which has permitted him to create birds that have directional feathering (feathers that grow outwards as well as upwards on the head). Also in Europe, as far as type is concerned, there are many really excellent specimens in the UK. Compared with years ago, Opalines have improved greatly in terms of type, but with markings it is another story. As Opalines have improved as Budgerigars (size, head, face, type, feathering), it has become more difficult to meet the marking requirements laid down for the variety.

What is the best way of breeding a good Opaline or Opaline Cinnamon?

Eric and Michael Lane:

We always try to pair best with best but if this does not work we try a brother of the best cock to the best hen or a sister of the best hen to the best cock. We never pair Opaline Light Green with Opaline Light Green or Opaline Skyblue with Opaline Skyblue because such pairings lose depth of body colour. The same is true of Opaline Cinnamon Light Greens and Skyblues. The best partner for an Opaline Skyblue is an Opaline Grey Green. From this pairing you can get four different coloured Opalines, Light Greens, Skyblues, Grey Greens and Greys. We have bred some very nice Opalines this way. We pair Opaline hens with our Normal cocks, most of which are split for Opaline. Many breeders use Opalines to improve spot size on Normals and, in our opinion, Opalines seem to be more fertile than Normals, these days. Cousin to cousin is as close as we pair, though in the past we have tried closer relationships. The results were disappointing with some of the chicks being as small as pet-types. You do hear of exceptions to this. I recall reading an article by Dr Robertson of South Africa who was forced to make very close pairings because he could not obtain outcrosses. His results were very good. However, with a stud as large as ours there is never any need to go closer than we wish.

Jim Hutton:

As with all livestock, you must pair best to best – as long as they are not both carrying the same fault. I believe this to be more important with birds than with larger animals. Because I have a small stud I have to be very

An Opaline Grey Green cock bred by Eric and Michael Lane.

selective and will not use any bird that is not a good example of the species. This means that birds with faults are discarded and the ratio of good birds produced is relatively high. This does not mean that every bird produced is a worldbeater, but it does mean that the youngsters produced are of a fairly high standard and so capable of producing outstanding progeny. There are not many outstanding Budgerigars produced in any one year, with luck playing a major part, so the more assistance you can give the better the odds become. Over the years, Cinnamons have had a reputation for being short of feather. Although I do not agree with this, I still avoid using any bird that is lacking in feather. It was once thought that Feather Dusters were the result of pairing buff Budgerigars together. This is nonsense: they are genetic freaks. I have no hesitation in pairing buff with buff though, as with all things, there is a limit to how far you can go. There is no point in producing Budgerigars with feather so long that they become unbalanced. There is a stage when buff feathering might be considered to be a fault and so not to be paired with another of its own type. You always need to be planning for the future. Pairings are not just for the immediate year, they must be looking two or three years ahead. If you feel your stud might be losing size you need to bring in a large outcross – but not any old large bird will do. It must be compatible with your own bloodline. How close can you breed? I know one top breeder who did well from a half-brother to half-sister pairing. But, in my view, such a pairing can only be a one off. Continuing on those lines is a shortcut to failure. When a family is producing particularly good progeny it is worth trying uncle to niece, aunt to nephew and cousin to cousin pairings put pairing closely-related Budgerigars on a regular basis can lead to a lot of problems.

Roy Aplin:

There are people, with deep pockets, who come into the Fancy and – because of the quality of the stock they can afford – breed a quality Budgerigar in their first year. However, deep pockets don't bring knowledge. Setting up a STUD of quality is an entirely different matter – and takes many years. There are basic rules to follow: 1) continually balance bad points with good, 2) if you see a particular fault establishing itself go out and get an outcross to correct it and 3) don't believe everything you are told. In my early days I was advised never to pair Opaline Cinnamon with Opaline Cinnamon because I would lose size, yet combined with a programme of continuous balancing this is the pairing that has bred some of my best Opaline Cinnamons. You need to be prepared to experiment. I have heard it

One of the breeding cages where Roy Aplin breeds his winners.

said that it is best not to introduce Opaline Cinnamons into a stud of Lutinos, yet in the 1960s Charles Hayter used this pairing to produce some of the best Lutinos I have ever seen. Listen to the theories, but until you have tried them out you will never know if they are true. Feather type must always be in your mind if you are trying to breed top quality exhibition Budgerigars. The 1980s were dominated by "feather" but many birds became too coarse and lost their style and their fertility. Most top breeders aim for intermediate rather than coarse feathering these days. Whatever the relationship of Budgerigars they must have compatible features before you can consider pairing them together. Cousin to cousin is a good pairing but I have bred many challenge certificate winners from grandfather to grand-daughter pairings. The problems, these days, is that the short life expectancy of top-quality exhibition Budgerigars can derail such plans.

Dr Alf Robertson:

The best pairings, as far as I am concerned, are Opaline x Opaline and Normal/Opaline cock x Opaline hen – provided that their backs are reasonably clean and their masks have depth. There are always plenty of useful Normal/Opaline cocks in my stud, because I regularly use Normal cocks paired with Opaline hens to improve the Normal side of the stud. (The outcome of these pairings can be found in chapter 7) I am a great believer in inbreeding. To some extent this course was forced on me because, in the early days, it was impossible to purchase quality Budgerigars in South Africa and it was expensive to import birds from Europe. In consequence, I had to set about fixing the good points of the Farmer, Finey and Byles Budgerigars that I had already imported. So I used such matings as half-brother to half-sister, uncle to niece and aunt to nephew. The results I achieved proved that inbreeding works and I am now convinced that the pairings I have just mentioned are the best.

How would you advise a newcomer to Opaline and Opaline Cinnamons to set up a successful stud?

Eric and Michael Lane:

If we were newcomers, wanting to set up a stud, we would go to a well-known fancier to buy five or six pairs. We would be looking only for the cheapest birds available and we would see how we got on with these for a couple of years. It is highly likely – because the birds would have come from good bloodlines – that some progress would be made in those two years. We would then go back to the same breeder and buy one or two better birds and carry on in this way until we were breeding good quality. That is the way we did it. We stuck to buying Budgerigars from Harry Bryan. We never bought from anyone else. When Harry started asking us for the odd bird we knew we had good stock. We would not start off with "fancy" colours such as Clearwings, Spangles, Recessive Pieds, Albinos, Lutinos and the like. It would be far better to keep to Normals, Opalines, Cinnamons and Opaline Cinnamons, to start with.

Jim Hutton:

It is perhaps more difficult for a newcomer to start a stud today than it has ever been. There are fewer top studs around, nowadays, than ever before. As a result there are very few quality Budgerigars on the market. The birds that ARE for sale may have been bred from the right lines but, visually, they are not what most people are looking for. Nevertheless, I will explain what I would do if I was new to the hobby and wanted to start a stud of Opaline Cinnamons. First, I would visit as many shows as possible and study the winning Opaline Cinnamons so that I understood what made a good one. I would check who was winning in the young bird classes and visit them to assess the overall quality of the stud to make sure that they were not winning with just the same few birds. If the quality was there I would ask what was for sale. I would not expect to buy winners, rather their brothers and sisters. I would hope to buy two pairs of Opaline Cinnamons, containing either two brothers or two sisters. Colour is unimportant, Grey, Blue, Green, they are all compatible. If I was lucky enough to get both pairs to breed I would take two rounds and then change over the pairings for a late, breeding round in an attempt to get half-brothers and half-sisters. I would start the second year by pairing the progeny of the initial rounds in cousin to cousin matings. For the third year I would have second-cousins and the progeny of the first year's late round to give plenty of choice. Improvements should be detected - perhaps not dramatic improvements - but enough to show that I was on the right lines. When the chicks from all the pairings start to display a family resemblance I would know that I was really on my way. It is better that a stud should develop in this way, with many capable of winning specials in a lower section rather than breeding a couple that take best in show awards - with nothing to back them up. At some stage I would introduce a Yellowface to add classes to my show potential.

Roy Aplin:

Anyone starting off in the hobby needs one year learning how to care for and breed Budgerigars. For this, it is not necessary to have birds of exhibition quality. While gaining this experience, join a local society and hope to meet a genuine fancier who has the knowledge and experience to provide the right sort of guidance to get you off to a good start. Start off with four to six pairs from, say, two breeders; not from here, there and everywhere.

Eric Lane is happy to breed a winner at any time of the year.

Jim Hutton keeps young birds in this inside flight.

Colour is not important, but there can be no doubt that brightly-coloured Budgerigars – Blues and Pieds – are easier to sell to bring in money to pay for seed. If, at the end of the first serious year of breeding, some of the youngsters are better than their parents you will be doing well. The next stage is to assess your stock to determine what features need to be improved. If the mask spots are too small, go out and find a Budgerigar with large spots, preferably set on a deep, wide mask. Putting all the pieces together over a period of years is far more satisfying than going out and buying the complete Budgerigar – if you can find one!

Dr Alf Robertson:

I would advise starting by obtaining three pairs from a successful top breeder, making sure that they are related to his best birds. The objective then is to breed as many chicks as possible. In the first year, switch a couple of the pairs over so that there will be a supply of half-brothers and half-sisters for the second breeding season. In the second year I would pair the fathers to their best daughters and the mothers to their best sons. Half-brother to half-sister pairings would also be employed. By the third year a gene pool will have been established and the best birds should be paired together.

How important is it for you to ring chicks at the earliest possible time?

Eric and Michael Lane:

Theoretically speaking, we would prefer to pair up so that the first chicks are ready to be ringed when the official rings arrive, after New Years Day. In practice, we achieve this a lot of the time, but if a particular pair seems ready to breed at ANY time of the year, we pair them up. We believe that bringing the official ring issue date forward to November 1 would result in more Budgerigars being bred.

Jim Hutton:

With shows starting in early July, pressure builds up to have chicks ready to ring in early January. I have reached the time of life when I ignore such pressures, in the knowledge that there are always later shows. One show is as good as another to me and, as far as I am concerned, it is best to pair Budgerigars when they are fit – regardless of the time of the year.

Roy Aplin:

I like to have a few young Budgerigars ready for the early shows and so put down a few pairs at the end of October – though it can be quite frustrating when you miss ringing a really promising youngster with the new year's rings. In my experience, most Budgerigars are ready to breed at that time of the year, to some extent because of the weather conditions. Although the ancestors of our domesticated Budgerigars came from a hot climate, today's Budgerigars seem to prefer a cooler environment. Many British breeders still have their Budgerigars paired up in May, when the weather is hotting up. In my experience, Budgerigars that are breeding in hot weather become lethargic and do not feed well, particularly in a wooden birdroom. A brick-built structure remains much cooler inside. Someone is bound to point to the good Budgerigars that are bred in the hot climate of Brazil, but it is much more humid there and that could well make a difference.

Dr Alf Robertson:

The problem of trying to get chicks in the nest when the official closed rings arrive does not arise in South Africa. Young bird classes cater not only for current-year Budgerigars, but also for those wearing the previous year's rings. I hear that there are Budgerigar breeders in the UK who would like the ring issue date to be brought forward from January 1. Adopting the South African system could solve some of the problems.

How do you go about acquiring stock of the required quality?

Eric and Michael Lane:

We are lucky enough to have the sort of relationships with other breeders which permit us exchange birds on a "breeding loan" system. We exchange birds just for the breeding season and then they return to their original homes. In the past, we have purchased birds we have seen and liked. It didn't matter whether they had been bred by champions or beginners. Some fanciers who have had birds from us are doing really well so if we want to get hold of birds that come from our own bloodline we know where to go. In our view, that is a good way of staying at the top.

Jim Hutton:

Because my stud is small I have to be extremely selective so the standard of stock I require is very high. There are few breeders in Britain who are prepared to sell exceptional Budgerigars and they are even more reluctant when the person they are selling to is going to be showing against them. Until 1992 I exchanged birds and often felt I had the worst of the deal. In 1992 I swopped with a breeder from Cornwall and was very happy with the deal. Since then I have been lucky enough to buy stock birds with the features I require. The prices, although not cheap, were not outrageous.

Roy Aplin:

When you are working with a line of Budgerigars you occasionally find it needs a boost and so you must bring in an outcross. As a champion breeder this is not always easy but, by maintaining good relationships with other fanciers, I usually manage to buy or exchange a bird when I need to.

Dr Alf Robertson:

Since the 1960s, all of the Budgerigars I have brought into the stud have come from Brian Byles.

Do you ever sell the best Opalines and Opaline Cinnamons from your stud?

Eric and Michael Lane:

Top quality exhibition Budgerigars are harder to breed today than ever before, so no-one is going to anxious to let them go. We might part with a good cock - if we have had two good breeding seasons from it and have birds just as good to take its place. It often takes two years to get the best out of an outstanding bird because, unless you find the right hen, they can sometimes produce disappointing youngsters.

Jim Hutton:

I do not see how you can make progress by retaining old stock so I always let even my best birds go after two breeding seasons and two show seasons. If I have not achieved the best possible results in the breeding room in two years I am unlikely to do it in later years. What satisfaction is there in exhibiting a bird that always takes best in show if there is nothing to back it up?

Roy Aplin:

No, I do not sell my best Budgerigars. They take years to develop but only seconds to sell. If you are in the hobby for enjoyment, then you need good-quality Budgerigars around you. That having been said, there

A young Opaline Cinnamon Light Green hen from Roy Aplin's birdroom.

ARE times – after finding your best bird dead on the floor of the cage – when you wonder why you did not accept the offer that you refused without consideration!

Dr Alf Robertson:

Never! A true fancier never sells his best birds.

What, in your opinion, is the degree of difficulty of Opalines and Opaline Cinnamons?

Eric and Michael Lane:

Opalines are one of the hardest varieties to breed to high standards. The problem is that there are so many areas in which they can be faulted on their markings (ticked heads, dirty backs, smudged wing markings) over and above the physical faults that are common to every variety. Budgerigars showing marking faults can be used in the breeding programme but it must always be remembered that the objective is clean heads, clean backs and distinct wing markings with the wing background colour the same as the body.

Jim Hutton:

The difficulty in ANY stud is maintaining quality. I am convinced that Budgerigars would revert to the wild type if left to their own devices. With Opaline Cinnamons, assuming you have maintained size and deportment, you have to keep checking their markings. The density of the wing markings must be maintained and so must a clear back: the most difficult feature of all Opalines. Nothing looks worse than an Opaline Cinnamon with a dirty back.

Roy Aplin:

In most respects, Opalines and Opaline Cinnamons are no more difficult or any easier than any other variety of Budgerigar. You need to work hard to maintain head quality, depth of mask, width of shoulder, deportment and good, round spots. Once the Opaline factor enters into the equation, you also need to keep heads free from flecking and the area between the wing butts as clear as possible of markings.

Dr Alf Robertson:

In my experience, Opalines are easy to breed – but difficult to breed to the written standard.

Are there any tactics that can help you win with Opalines and Opaline Cinnamons?

Eric and Michael Lane:

There are no tactics, as such, that will help a bird to win. The secret is to have an excellent specimen to put in the show cage. The sort of Opaline or Opaline Cinnamon you want will be of good size, standing well off the perch as it looks the judge in the eye, have a good wide, clean head which it will raise to show extra height, a clean back, even, deep body colour, clear wing markings and bright eyes – the perfect Opaline. Years ago, we used to put out really big show teams. I remember putting four young Grey cocks in the same class at the BS Club Show in 1978. They were placed first, second, fourth and seventh in a very strong class. The winner went on to take the awards for best breeder in show and best Budgerigar in show. At that same, 1978, event we benched the best opposite sex in show and second-best any age in show. At a BS Club Show in the 1980s we entered five Opaline Cinnamon cocks in the same class and they were placed first, second, third,

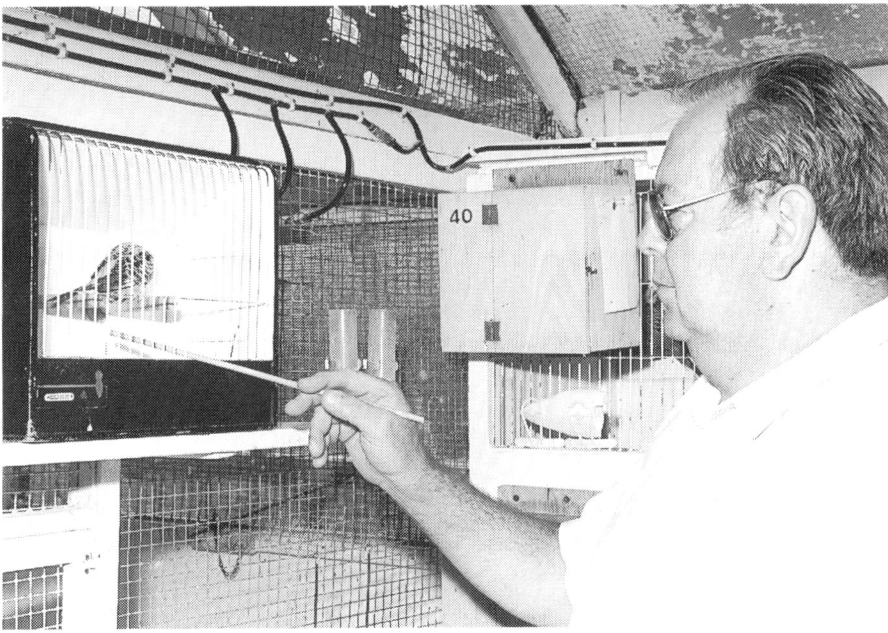

Eric Lane puts this young Opaline through the training process.

fifth and seventh. In those days we used to fill two cars with show cages and in the days when the BS Club Show was held in Leicester we were permitted to deliver birds on the morning of the show. We were often caging up birds at 3 o'clock in the morning! It was hard work, but they were happy days. These days we tend to enter not more than two Budgerigars in the same class.

Jim Hutton:

The best advice is to always ensure that your Budgerigars are properly presented at shows. The birds themselves must be clean, showing no broken feathers and have well-trimmed masks. Deportment can be bred into a stud but training is still important: these features plus excellent presentation can make a fairly good Budgerigar into a prize winner. Although it is not wise to show a Budgerigar that is in anything but tip-top condition a really outstanding specimen can overcome the absence of the odd feather. I remember taking best in show with an Opaline Cinnamon Light Green cock at Western Counties Area Championship, even though it was missing a spot. On the other hand, I missed out with an equally good bird at another show because it would not perch while being judged. That shows how important training is. It should start in the nest, with every chick being handled every day. They learn that there is nothing to be afraid of and soon learn to behave properly in a show cage. A disadvantage of a small stud is that you do not have as many birds to choose from when selecting the show team. However, whenever possible I like to enter two birds in each class. This increases the chance of winning as it helps to eradicate the problem of a judge taking a dislike to one, particular exhibit. But even winning is not always the end of the story. Back in 1967 I bred an outstanding Opaline Cinnamon cock late in the season; possibly one of the best I have ever bred. It was at the time you could send birds to shows by rail. I sent him to the Scottish National and he was best Budgerigar in show. I opened the box when it arrived home and found the cage and the rosettes – but the bird had disappeared.

Roy Aplin:

Some people have the skill to breed a top-class Budgerigar but lack the ability to show it at its best. When a Budgerigar goes onto the show bench it should be as near 100 per cent perfect as possible. It must be clean (from spraying and hand-washing the feathers above the cere) and its mask must be well trimmed. If a bird is worthy of a top award, its cage should complement it. Always stage an excellent Budgerigar in an immaculate show cage. It can be interesting to enter three Budgerigars in the same class, particularly if they are different types of birds. You can often be surprised when the bird you least expected comes home with a top award – because the judge does not see Budgerigars in the same way that you do.

Dr Alf Robertson:

First of all, you must have a good example of the variety, but there is more to it than that. Show preparation and training can make all of the difference when it comes to taking top prizes. Harry Bryan demonstrated special skills in this direction and you only have to look at the success he has achieved, over the years, to see how much it counts. When exhibiting, I like to put two or three birds in each class. This helps to make allowances for a judge's particular preferences.

How do you go about judging Opalines and Opaline Cinnamons?

Eric and Michael Lane:

Whatever variety I am judging, I walk along the line of birds and pick out the ones with the best heads. I take them out of the line and put them towards the head of the class. I then place them in order, taking into account both the general points that apply to all Budgerigars and the specific points that apply to the variety in question. All of the birds that were rejected at the initial selection stage are compared with the top seven before being rejected completely or, on further consideration, make it into the cards. Any bird with an undershot beak is thrown out and any showing signs of scaly face are removed from the show hall. I particularly dislike Budgerigars with narrow heads and head flecking so these are very heavily penalised. I think I am a fair judge and believe this is the general view because I receive lots of invitations to judge, year after year. Most of the judges I know are quite competent when judging Opalines and Opaline Cinnamons. There are, however, a few who will never make good judges and most of these are people who keep the rarer varieties and do not recognise a good Budgerigar when they see it. They are happier judging their own speciality. That is why some judges have difficulty getting engagements. When we have to show Opalines and Opaline Cinnamons under such judges we cross our fingers and hope for the best. Some judges seem to be opposed to Opalines and Opaline Cinnamons. They always seem to vote for a Normal. This is unfortunate because they should realise that it is more difficult to breed a good Opaline than a good Normal and give credit where credit is due. Another group of judges seem willing to vote only for a bird that they have previously judged in the classes – as though there is some reflected glory in having put up the best in show. The Budgerigar Society colour standards for Opalines and Opaline Cinnamons are quite adequate.

Jim Hutton:

When judging, I like to stand back so that I can take a good look at the whole class. I then select seven or eight that appeal to me most. I don't try to put them in any particular order at this stage, but turn my attention to the rest of the exhibits. Are they as good as the selected seven or eight? I keep the best of them back in case I have to reject one of the first-chosen because, on closer examination, it has a fault (for example, missing flights or tail). I now begin placing them in order. The first things I look for are face and head qualities, width of shoulder, deportment (it is very important that they stand up, looking proud) and a good lift of head feathers. Good width of head is essential. This is where lateral feathering each side of the cere plays such an important part. Whichever bird I decide to put first must be in condition, making allowances for the fact that a large buff will never be as tight-feathered as a short-feathered Budgerigar. Up to now, the judging technique I have described applies to any variety – I go for quality every time. However, with Opaline Cinnamons I have further checks to make. Is the body colour solid rather than wishy-washy? Does the bird have a reasonably clean back? Are the wing markings well defined? If I can answer "Yes" to those questions I am close to putting up a worthy winner. When exhibiting Opaline Cinnamons I am not too concerned whether the judge keeps the variety himself. A good judge will always reward quality. There are a few judges who I am not keen on exhibiting under. These are the

Flecked Budgerigars always present problems for judges.

types who, never having bred one, cannot recognise the modern Budgerigar. They are more likely to choose a small, tight-feathered bird in excellent feather than a larger, looser-feather Budgerigar of quality. The standard of points laid down by the Budgerigar Society for Opaline Cinnamons is very fair though the fact is that judges in Britain only take points into account when two exhibits are so closely matched that they need to find some way of separating them.

Roy Aplin:

As a Budgerigar Society panel judge, I regularly get the opportunity to judge Opalines and Opaline Cinnamons. As with any other variety, a large class always poses a challenge. Birds displaying good head qualities and excellent depth of mask can catch your attention straight away, but I am always on the look-out for stylish deportment and head capping that is free of flecking. Today, it is rare to find an Opaline or Opaline Cinnamon of quality that has a clean back, but a judge's job is to select the best from the exhibits that are placed before him. There is no excuse for any judge not being able to judge every variety of Budgerigar. In the unlikely event of you accepting an engagement and then finding that you been allocated a colour or variety that you are not sure about, it is your duty to fill in the gaps in your knowledge before the day of the show. No matter how much you study the varieties, there can be rare occasions when an exhibit comes before you that causes problems of identification. Consultation with the other judges usually solves the problem. When passing opinions about judges, you must realise that we are not professionals. We are merely following one aspect of our hobby, to the best of our ability. But, having said that, I have to admit that not all judges work to the scale of points laid down by the Budgerigar Society. The Ideal standard could be changed to reflect the points displayed by today's top Budgerigars (large heads and deep masks) but if you start making changes where would it end?

Dr Alf Robertson:

When judging, the first thing I look for is type. I do not immediately throw out Opalines that display slight head ticking, nor do I reject those with slightly-marked backs. I DO immediately reject any exhibit that has poor type. I then set about assessing the exhibits, penalising all of the known Opaline marking faults. In this way, an Opaline that combines good type and markings that approximate to the standard comes out on top. When showing, I am quite happy to exhibit under judges who do not keep Opalines themselves.

How do you see the future of Opalines and Opaline Cinnamons?

Eric and Michael Lane:

There is no doubt that, in the first half of the 1990s, the numbers of Opalines and Opaline Cinnamons being exhibited were lower than the varieties deserve. There have been some very good ones around, but not in the numbers seen in previous years. Most breeders of Normals use Opalines and Opaline Cinnamons to improve and maintain certain desirable features – such as overall size, spot size and fertility – and we wish they would go one step further and start breeding them for exhibition.

Jim Hutton:

A good Opaline Cinnamon is a very good Budgerigar and, as long as this remains the case, I cannot see the variety losing its popularity. Beginners and novices, particularly, tend to follow fashion – to be influenced by what is successful – and so if an Opaline Cinnamon was to take the supreme award at the Budgerigar Society Club Show I would expect to see many more bred and exhibited.

The future of Opaline and Opaline Cinnamon Budgerigars will come from inside these nestboxes for Roy Aplin.

Roy Aplin:

Opalines and Opaline Cinnamons have gone through a subdued spell because of the dominance of Normals - but I think they are on their way back - particularly Opaline Cinnamons! Lots of studs in the UK contain Opaline Cinnamons but they are wasted by being paired with Normals. If only more breeders would pair Opaline with Opaline they would soon increase in numbers and quality. There was a time when Opaline Cinnamons dominated the show scene but Normal Grey Greens pushed them into the background. If I can succeed with Opalines, there is no reason why other breeders cannot do the same. At the time of writing I am making an analysis of pedigrees to establish just how my best Opalines and Opalines Cinnamons were bred, so that I can repeat the combinations of bloodlines that did the trick previously. So watch out!

Dr Alf Robertson:

Although the latest Budgerigar Society colour standard are an improvement on those that preceded them, we are still left with the problem that Opalines are more difficult to breed to the Ideal standard than Normals. Having said that, the future of Opalines is safe - if only because they are so useful for improving other varieties.

There is always another year–Roy Aplin prepares the breeding cages.

CHAPTER 7

COLOUR EXPECTATIONS

The subject of Budgerigar colour expectations could fill a book on its own – in fact it HAS filled a book and anyone who wants to delve deeper into the subject should read Taylor and Warner's *Genetics for Budgerigar Breeders.* Understanding genetics CAN help, when it comes to breeding good Budgerigars and controlling the numbers of particular varieties – particularly when sex-linked varieties, such as Opaline and Cinnamon are involved. However, if you find the subject difficult to understand you will be in good company, and should not worry unduly. For the benefit of those who are interested, and to assist understanding of some of the recommended pairings, there follows a description of how sex-linked colour expectations can be calculated.

The first fact that needs to be understood is that, in every case, there are TWO factors controlling every individual colour and variety. In this book, the letters used to denote these are not necessarily the ones that are used in serious text books, but have been chosen to make it easier for the inexperienced to understand. Some breeders' first contact with genetics comes when they hear the term "sex-linked" – often accompanied by dire warnings that could put anyone off keeping Budgerigars! There is no need to harbour any fears. "Sex-linked" just means that the variety and sex of a Budgerigar are directly connected.

Before going on to specific varieties, let us examine how the sex of a chick is determined. TWO factors control sex and when two Budgerigars mate, each gives ONE of its colour factors and ONE of its sex factors to each chick. The possible combinations can be represented by a grid of four squares. In this case there is no better way than using the approved letters; "X" and "Y". When two "X"s combine you have a cock bird. When it is an "X" and a "Y" that come together you have a hen. So "XX" is a cock and "XY" is a hen. Using the grid, we can find out what happens when a cock mates with a hen.

		Cock	
		X	X
Hen	X	XX	XX
	Y	XY	XY

Not surprisingly, the result is half cocks and half hens.

Sex-linked varieties, like Opaline and Cinnamon, can attach themselves only to the "X" factor. To explain the principle, let us use Opaline as the working example An Opaline factor can be denoted "Xo". An Opaline cock is then represented by "XoXo" and an Opaline hen by "XoY". There are three possibilities for cocks; "XoXo" (Opaline), "XX" (Non-Opaline) and "XoX" (Non-Opaline split Opaline). For hens there are just two; "XoY" (Opaline) or "XY" (Non-Opaline). Only cocks can be split for sex-linked factors such as Opaline.

Because sex-linkage causes problems to so many people it is worth checking a number of Opaline matings (remember, you can substitute any of the other sex-linked varieties, such as Cinnamon). Opaline to Opaline produces all Opalines and Non-Opaline to Non-Opaline produces all Non-Opalines so we can move quickly on to the remaining possibilities, starting with Opaline cock x Non-Opaline hen:

		Opaline Cock	
		Xo	Xo
Non-Opaline Hen	X	XoX	XoX
	Y	XoY	XoY

All cocks are "XoX" (Non-Opaline split Opaline) and all hens a "XoY" (Opaline).

Next, we can check what happens when a Non-Opaline cock is paired with an Opaline hen.

		Non-Opaline Cock	
		X	X
Opaline Hen	Xo	XoX	XoX
	Y	XY	XY

All cocks are, again, "XoX" (Non-Opaline split Opaline) but this time all hens are "XY" (Non-Opaline). No visual Opalines are produced from this pairing.

Now, Non-Opaline split Opaline cock x Opaline hen

		Non-Opaline/Opaline Cock X	Non-Opaline/Opaline Cock Xo
Opaline Hen	Xo	XoX	XoXo
	Y	XY	XoY

This mating throws up an interesting mixture. Cocks are either Opaline or Non-Opaline split Opaline, while hens are Opaline or Non-Opaline.

Finally, we come to the mating that causes most of the confusion; Non-Opaline split Opaline cock x Non-Opaline hen.

		Non-Opaline/Opaline Cock X	Non-Opaline/Opaline Cock Xo
Non-Opaline Hen	X	XX	XXo
	Y	XY	XoY

Cocks are either Non-Opaline or Non-Opaline split Opaline, while the hens are Non-Opaline or Opaline. So from a mating in which neither partner is a visual Opaline, a proportion of the chicks produced (all hens) ARE Opalines!

As indicated earlier, merely by substituting Cinnamon for Opaline (Xc instead of Xo) and carrying out exactly the same exercises all of the possible expectations from Cinnamons can be calculated. However, this book is about Opaline Cinnamons not Normal Cinnamons, so these need to be considered next.

The fact that we can refer to Opaline Cinnamons shows that two sex-linked factors (in this case Opaline and Cinnamon) can be carried by the same bird at the same time, but they need not necessarily be carried on the same X chromosome. XcoX and XcXo both signify a cock that is split for Opaline Cinnamon; the first being known as Type I and the second as Type II. But that need not worry us at the level of genetics which we are considering. Suffice it to say that, because of a happening called the "crossover", both Type I and Type II produce the same practical breeding results – with a slight difference in the numbers of each variety bred.

It will be appreciated that charting all of the possible combinations would take up many pages and so – as this chapter provides all the tools you need to work out colour expectations of sex-linked Budgerigars – we will conclude with three simplified tables which show the varieties of chicks you can expect from pairings involving Opalines and Opaline Cinnamons.

TABLE 1 Matings involving Opalines and Non-Opalines.

(Note: for the purpose of this table any variety that is not an Opaline (Normal, Cinnamon, Spangle, Pied, Clearwing, etc. is referred to as "Normal".) The Red-eye mutations (Lutino and Albino) have the ability to mask the markings carried by other varieties. For further explanation read "All about Red-eye Budgerigars", from this series.)

Parents		Youngsters	
Cock	Hen	Cocks	Hens
Opaline	Opaline	Opaline	Opaline
Opaline	Normal	Normal/Opaline	Opaline
Normal	Opaline	Normal/Opaline	Normal
Normal/Opaline	Opaline	Opaline Normal/Opaline	Opaline Normal
Normal/Opaline	Normal	Normal/Opaline Normal	Opaline Normal
Normal	Normal	Normal	Normal

TABLE 2 Matings involving Opaline Cinnamons and Non-Opaline Cinnamons

(*Note: for the purpose of this table any variety that is not an Opaline Cinnamon (Normal, Spangle, Pied, Clearwing, etc. is referred to as "Normal".) The Red-eye mutations (Lutino and Albino) have the ability to mask the markings carried by other varieties. For further explanation read "All about Red-eye Budgerigars", from this series.*)

Parents		Youngsters	
Cock	Hen	Cocks	Hens
Opaline Cinnamon	Opaline Cin	Opaline Cinnamon	Opaline Cinnamon
Opaline Cinnamon	Normal	Normal/Opaline- -Cinnamon	Opaline Cinnamon
Normal	Opaline Cinnamon	Normal/Opaline- -Cinnamon	Normal
Normal/Opaline Cinnamon	Opaline Cinnamon	Opaline Cinnamon Normal/Opaline- -Cinnamon Cinnamon/Opaline Opaline/Cinnamon	Opaline Cinnamon Normal Cinnamon Opaline
Normal/Opaline Cinnamon	Normal	Normal/Opaline- -Cinnamon Normal Normal/Cinnamon Normal/Opaline	Opaline Cinnamon Normal Cinnamon Opaline
Normal	Normal	Normal	Normal

TABLE 3 A selection of matings involving Opaline Cinnamon and Opaline factors

(Note: for the purpose of this table any variety that is not an Opaline, Opaline Cinnamon or Cinnamon (Normal, Spangle, Pied, Clearwing, etc. is referred to as "Normal".) The Red- eye mutations (Lutino and Albino) have the ability to mask the markings carried by other varieties. For further explanation read "All about Red-eye Budgerigars", from this series.)

Parents		Youngsters	
Cock	Hen	Cocks	Hens
Opaline Cinnamon	Opaline	Opaline/Cinnamon	Opaline Cinnamon
Opaline	Opaline Cinnamon	Opaline/Cinnamon	Opaline
Opaline/Cinnamon	Opaline Cinnamon	Opaline Cinnamon Opaline/Cinnamon	Opaline Cinnamon Opaline
Opaline/Cinnamon	Opaline	Opaline Opaline/Cinnamon	Opaline Cinnamon Opaline
Opaline/Cinnamon	Cinnamon	Cinnamon/Opaline Normal/Opaline- -Cinnamon	Opaline Cinnamon Opaline
Opaline/Cinnamon	Normal	Normal/Opaline- -Cinnamon Normal/Opaline	Opaline Cinnamon Opaline
Normal/Opaline Cinnamon	Opaline Cinnamon	Opaline Cinnamon Normal/Opaline- -Cinnamon Cinnamon/Opaline Opaline/Cinnamon	Opaline Cinnamon Normal Cinnamon Opaline
Normal/Opaline Cinnamon	Opaline	Opaline/Cinnamon Normal/Opaline- -Cinnamon Opaline Normal/Opaline	Opaline Cinnamon Normal Cinnamon Opaline
Normal/Opaline Cinnamon	Cinnamon	Cinnamon/Opaline Normal/Cinnamon Cinnamon Normal/Opaline- -Cinnamon	Opaline Cinnamon Normal Cinnamon Opaline
Normal/Opaline Cinnamon	Normal	Normal/Opaline- -Cinnamon Normal Normal/Cinnamon Normal/Opaline	Opaline Cinnamon Normal Cinnamon Opaline

Further copies of this book and details about others in the "All about ..." series can be obtained from:

F. Wright,
31 Redford Avenue,
Wallington,
Surrey, SM6 9DT
United Kingdom.

Telephone or
Fax: 0181-647 6378

Ask for details of quantity and club discounts

Already in print:

All about Greens
All about Blues
All about Red-eyes
All about Greys and Grey Greens
All about Spangles
All about Opalines and Opaline Cinnamons

. . . and more are being prepared.

"The Budgerigar Man" The Harry Bryan way of breeding successful exhibition Budgerigars is still available from Fred Wright, at the above address. Price £9.95 plus £2 post and packing (£3 Overseas).

THE MAGAZINE FOR ALL BREEDERS, KEEPERS AND LOVERS OF BIRDS • THE MAGAZINE FOR ALL BREEDERS, KEEPERS AND LOVERS OF BIRDS